AMERICAN INDIAN VOICES

AMERICAN INDIAN VOICES

EDITED AND WITH
INTRODUCTION AND NOTES BY
KAREN D. HARVEY

Consultant: Lisa D. Harjo

Writers of America
THE MILLBROOK PRESS
BROOKFIELD, CONNECTICUT

JUNCA

Library of Congress Cataloging-in-Publication Data
American Indian voices/edited and with introduction and notes by
Karen Harvey; consultant, Lisa Harjo.
p.   cm.—(Writers of America)
Includes bibliographical references and index.
Summary: Includes songs and prayers, myths and legends,
biographical sketches, stories, poetry, and passages which capture
the traditions, beliefs, and history of native American peoples.
ISBN 1-56294-382-0
1. Indians of North America—Literary Collections.   2. American
literature—Indian authors.   [1. Indians of North America—Literary
collections.   2. American Literature—Indian authors—Collections.]
I. Harvey, Karen D.   II. Harjo, Lisa.   III. Series
PZ5.A5117   1994
810.8'0897—dc20   94-21418   CIP   AC

Published by The Millbrook Press, Inc.
2 Old New Milford Road, Brookfield, Connecticut 06804

To my parents,
Freeman Bernard and Constance Herndon Decker,
who encouraged my love of learning
and patiently allowed me
to find my own path.

Photographs courtesy of the Philbrook Museum, Tulsa, Okla.: pp. 12, 46, 106, 132; Native American Painting Reference Library: pp. 17, 39, 53, 64, 101; Denver Art Museum: pp. 22; Museum of Northern Arizona: p. 25 (Edward R. Curtis, plates supplementing Vol. I *North American Indians*, neg. #67.33); Museum of Indian Arts & Culture/Laboratory of Anthropology, Santa Fe: p. 31 (catalog #35464/13, photo by Blair Clark); Institute of American Indian Arts, Santa Fe: pp. 72, 77; U.S. Dept. of the Interior, Indian Arts and Crafts Board, Museum of the Plains Indian & Craft Center, Browning, Mont.: pp. 81, 109 (photos by Joe Fisher); Museum of the American Indian: p. 90; Bert Seabourn: p. 98.

Contents

AMERICAN INDIAN VOICES

Introduction

Grandfather,
a voice I am going to send.
Hear me.
All over the universe,
a voice I am going to send.
Hear me,
Grandfather.
I will live.
I have said it.

Opening Prayer of the Sun Dance[1]

More than two thousand native tribes were scattered throughout the Americas when Columbus landed in the West Indies in 1492. During the following five hundred years of European settlement, many of these tribes were either destroyed or seriously threatened by warfare, disease, missionary zeal, and government policies. About five hundred federally recognized tribes remain in the United States today. In spite of the centuries of loss and violent destruction of their cultures, American Indians are experiencing a surge of growth, pride, and renewal of traditions.

Columbus gave the people of this land the name "Indians." They have since been called by many names: Native Americans, American Indians, indigenous peoples, and even redskins. In their own languages, the names they have given themselves are often translated as "the People."

Cheyenne Sun Dance, First Painting of the Third Day, by Richard West (Cheyenne), 1949.

Although scholars often use the more formal terms, in everyday life many Native people call themselves Indians. They also prefer to be identified by their specific tribe, such as Navajo, Cherokee, Cheyenne, Apache, or Sioux.

Tribal identity is important because North American Indians are not part of a single culture. Just as Europeans, Asians, and Africans live within numerous separate countries, Indian people in America belong to many different nations, or tribes. Each of these nations has its own language and form of government as well as its unique culture and way of life.

Yet they are tied together through their shared beliefs and values. This common worldview creates a sense of "Indianness," whether the person is a Navajo from the Southwest, a Sioux from the Plains, or a Cherokee from the Southeast. Here are some of the perceptions about life that many Indians share:

All creations are interdependent; that is, all things are created for a purpose and human beings share this purpose. For this reason, it is important to maintain a natural balance between humans and their environment.

The Lakota People conclude their prayers with the words *mitakuye oyasin*, meaning "All my relations" or "We are all related." Prayer includes all creations of the universe. These words remind the Lakotas of their role in the whole of life and their responsibility to all creations.

Most American Indians believe in an ultimate Creator who is everywhere and can see, hear, and know everything. This Creator is addressed through prayer and ceremony with great reverence.

Religion and art are not separated from daily existence; they are integrated into the whole of life. A woman in times past would create an earthen pot in which to carry and store water. She would paint a symbol on the outside to represent water. She believed that if she was respectful of the role that water played in her life and aware of its natural laws, water would be plentiful. In this way, her art and religion were part of her daily life.

Language is more than a function; it is spiritual. While there are vast differences between Indian languages, this understanding of its spiritual meaning is shared. Words have power and are sacred. Words come from the center of the body where the heart and breath are. Words create a bond between humans and all creations.

Beyond the physical world is another world that some call the spirit world or the world of unseen powers. One world is not without the other, and both worlds are real. People—and all creations—are made of body and spirit. All creations are of the physical and spirit world. Indians' prayers, ceremonies, and songs call upon the spirits of the creations to come to their aid.[2]

The history of Native Americans is unlike that of other Americans. America has often been called a "melting pot," a nation formed by immigrants and refugees who came here to create a new way of life. Indians were not immigrants, though. This land had been theirs for thousands of years until foreigners came and eventually conquered them.

You will discover, as you read the origin stories included in the following pages, that many Indians believe they are from this earth; they belong to it. They are not immigrants; this earth is their mother.

Too frequently, the diversity of Indian people is reduced to a stereotype. They are thought of as noble savages, devout environmentalists, spiritual pacifists, or a vanishing people. Other times, they are thought of as brutal savages, destitute alcoholics, or humorless stoics. As people, they have a collective history, tribal differences, and individual experiences, hopes, and dreams. They also endure many of the same problems as other minority groups, and they have heroes, heroines, and triumphs as well. By reading American Indian literature—one of the most intriguing and satisfying ways to "walk in their moccasins"—it is possible to understand the hearts, spirits, and cultures of people of the past and present.

Long before Columbus encountered the "new world," Indians had a strong and rich oral literature. For centuries, myths and legends taught children what was right and wrong and how to live in the proper and sacred way. Stories helped to while away long winter evenings and taught important lessons as well. Songs and ceremonies helped to cure illness, bring rain, protect warriors, give thanks to the Creator, and ensure harmony and well-being.

One way that stories were remembered was through drawings and carvings on rocks. These pictographs and petroglyphs are preserved on the walls of caves and canyons and in other protected places. They are reminders of people who lived long ago.

Some tribes used strands of wampum, knots in a string, or paintings on rawhide as tools for remembering stories. Young people were given the responsibility—often with very rigorous training—of memorizing the stories and carrying them to the next generation.

Also within this oral tradition are the speeches given by Indian leaders who spoke out on behalf of their people. These speeches were given by people whose existence was threatened. They address matters of life and death with great urgency. Often the Indians had to decide to either resist the European and American intruders or give up their traditional lands. Through their speeches, it is possible to understand the issues that concerned American Indians in the past and the values that guided their decisions.

White historians and anthropologists began to record this

varied oral tradition, and they often transcribed the stories of Indian people as well. Many of these stories were told to someone who then wrote them down. Others were written down by Indians and then edited by non-Indian scholars. Eventually, personal stories were written by American Indian scholars themselves.

Still later, Indian writers began to write and publish in the standard American forms, including prose, fiction, poetry, and drama. Through these writings, the voices of Indians now speak to a larger audience and reflect Indian cultures as well as concerns shared by all human beings about the present and future.

This anthology has been organized to honor the voices of American Indian people. It will also honor the sacred number of four:

> Four is the number that is most wakan, most sacred. Four stands for Tatuye Topa—the four quarters of the earth. . . . Four, the sacred number, also stands for the four winds, whose symbol is the cross. . . . The Great Mystery Medicine Bag contained four times four things. . . . The bundle contained four kinds of skins from the birds, four kinds of fur from the animals, four kinds of plants, four kinds of rocks and stones. . . . Four things make the universe; earth, air, water, fire. . . . We set up four colored flags for all our ceremonies. . . . Red, white, black, yellow—these are the true colors. They give us the four directions; you might also say a trail toward our prayers.[3]

Four sections will be devoted to four recurring themes: the traditional beliefs of the People, their timeless traditions, the effect of change on individuals and tribes, and a celebra-

The Fourth World, by Andy Tsihnahjinnie (Navaho), about 1970.

tion of how American Indian peoples and cultures have survived. Within these themes of beliefs, traditions, change, and survival will appear many different forms of expression: songs and prayers, myths, legends, biographical sketches, stories, poetry, and passages from novels.

The central beliefs of American Indians relate to the interdependence of all life forms, reverence for and dependence upon the Creator, the relationship between body and spirit, and the everyday aspect of religion.

Traditions are behaviors that have been part of a culture for a long time. They are handed down by word of mouth or by example. Traditions can be part of a culture or a family. They are the threads that bind families and tribal cultures together.

Change refers to those things in our lives and surroundings that are in constant transition. For American Indians, change has frequently been an involuntary reaction to outside influence. Too often, change has been destructive.

In spite of conquest, removal from traditional lands, destruction of lifeways, and technological changes, Indian people and their cultures have survived. We have arrived at a time to celebrate Indian survival and the vigorous renewal of their cultures.

In the following pages, you will hear many American Indian voices speak of things that matter—beliefs, traditions, change, and survival.

PART ONE

BELIEFS

*The spoken word
is creation renewed.
Conceived in the mind
and born with the breath of life,
What I say to you is sacred.
These words are my creation, but always they are
My responsibility.
I choose not beauty nor anger,
but truth.*

Russell Boham, Oral Tradition[4]

Each culture answers basic questions about existence in different ways. These questions have to do with time, the relationships between people and between people and the environment, the purpose of day-to-day activity, and the nature of human beings. Am I more concerned with the past, the present, or the future? What is my relationship to the natural world? Do I conquer nature or live in harmony with it? What is the purpose of my life? Is it to achieve and acquire, or do I strive to lead a spiritual life? How do I relate to people? Are people basically good, bad, or neither? The way in which a culture answers these questions forms its unique worldview and the framework for the lifeways of its people.

The worldview of American Indians is so different from that of non-Indians that it takes a conscientious effort to understand and appreciate the beliefs that shape the Indian world. Traditional Indian ways of life are based upon interdependence, harmony, respect, and spirituality.

In general, Indian people live for today, not for tomorrow. Many tribes have no word for time and no need to be punctual because there is plenty of time. "Indian Time" generally means "late" in non-Indian time.

Saving and acquiring things for the future are not valued. People are respected for what they give, and a person who acquires material things is often feared.

Old age is not feared, it is respected. A trusted leader is usually an elder.

It is important to work together and share with others rather than to compete to be the best.

Harmony with nature and acceptance of the world are central to life. No attempt is made to change things. If rain doesn't fall or crops don't grow, it is because the necessary harmony has been destroyed. When it has been restored, nature will respond in kind.

And yet, cultures do not exist in isolation. This has been especially true for Indian peoples. For more than five hundred years they have been exposed to European cultures and forced to weaken or let go of many of their traditional beliefs.

Harvest Dance by Awa Tsireh/Alphonso Roybal (San Ildefonso Pueblo), early 1920s.

Indian children have been sent to boarding schools far from their family homes; tribes have been moved from traditional homelands to reservations; many people have moved into large urban areas; and missionaries have tried to convert the people to Christianity. Television and technology have been powerful influences on young people, who are tempted to become more "American" and less "Indian."

Many Indians have forgotten the old ways or chosen to adopt the beliefs and ways of non-Indian people. Others continue to practice their traditional beliefs. It is important to see Indians as individuals with many different voices.

When you read the following words of American Indian people, try to suspend judgment and to understand with both your head and your heart.

▼

JOY HARJO (CREEK)

Recognized as one of the most gifted writers of her generation, Joy Harjo is a poet, filmmaker, artist, teacher, and television scriptwriter. She considers herself a late bloomer, beginning to write when poetry became more "magical" to her than painting.

REMEMBER

Remember the sky that you were born under,
know each of the star's stories.
Remember the moon, know who she is. I met her
in a bar once in Iowa City.

Remember the sun's birth at dawn, that is the
strongest point of time. Remember sundown
and the giving away to night.
Remember your birth, how your mother struggled
to give you form and breath. You are evidence of
her life, and her mother's, and hers.
Remember your father, his hands cradling
your mother's flesh, and maybe her heart, too
and maybe not.
He is your life, also.
Remember the earth whose skin you are.
Red earth yellow earth white earth brown earth
black earth we are earth.
Remember the plants, trees, animal life who all
have their tribes, their families, their histories, too.
Talk to them, listen to them. They are alive poems.
Remember the wind. Remember her voice. She
knows the origin of this universe. I heard her
singing Kiowa war dance songs at the corner of
Fourth and Central once.
Remember that you are all people and that all people
are you.
Remember that you are this universe and that this
universe is you.
Remember that all is in motion, is growing, is you.
Remember that language comes from this.
Remember the dance that language is, that life is.
Remember
to remember.

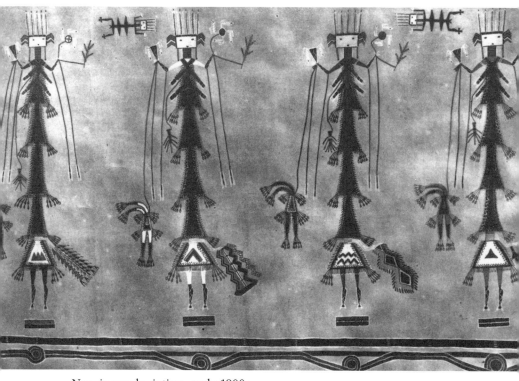

Navajo sandpainting, early 1900s.

The Night Chant is a nine-day Navajo healing ceremony conducted by a singer or chanter for the benefit of a "patient." The ceremony begins at sunset and ends eight and a half days later at sunrise. During the first part of the ceremony the patient is purified and makes offerings to the gods. At midnight of the fourth day the sleeping gods awake and descend from their homes to appear in the sandpainting. It is through the sandpaintings that they touch their bodies to the patient's body, giving the patient their power. The following selection is part of the ceremony that takes place during the final day and is sung by the patient.

A NAVAJO NIGHT CHANT

Happily I recover.
Happily my interior becomes cool.
Happily my eyes regain their power.
Happily my head becomes cool.
Happily my limbs regain their power.
Happily I hear again.
Happily for me *the spell* is taken off.
Happily may I walk.
Impervious to pain, may I walk.
Feeling light within, may I walk.
With lively feelings, may I walk.
Happily abundant dark clouds I desire.
Happily dark mists I desire.
Happily abundant passing showers I desire.
Happily an abundance of vegetation I desire.
Happily an abundance of pollen I desire.
Happily abundant dew I desire.
Happily may fair white corn, to the ends of the earth,
    come with you.
Happily may fair blue corn, to the ends of the earth,
    come with you.
Happily may fair corn of all kinds, to the ends of the earth,
    come with you.
Happily may fair plants of all kinds, to the ends of the earth,
    come with you.
Happily may fair goods of all kinds, to the ends of the earth,
    come with you.

Happily may fair jewels of all kinds, to the ends of the earth,
    come with you.
With these before you, happily may they come with you.
With these behind you, happily may they come with you.
With these below you, happily may they come with you.
With these above you, happily may they come with you.
With these all around you, happily may they come with you.
Thus happily you accomplish your tasks.
Happily the old men will regard you.
Happily the old women will regard you.
Happily the young men will regard you.
Happily the boys will regard you.
Happily the girls will regard you.
Happily the children will regard you.
Happily, as they scatter in different directions, they will
    regard you.
Happily as they approach their homes, they will regard you.
Happily may their roads home be on the trail of pollen.
Happily may they all get back.
In beauty I walk.
With beauty before me, I walk.
With beauty behind me, I walk.
With beauty below me, I walk.
With beauty above me, I walk.
With beauty all around me, I walk.
It is finished in beauty,
It is finished in beauty,
It is finished in beauty,
It is finished in beauty.

▼

ANNA L. WALTERS
(PAWNEE-OTOE)

Anna Lee Walters was born in Pawnee, Oklahoma, in 1946. A poet and prose writer, she has spent much of her life teaching at Navajo Community College in Tsaile, Arizona. She is coauthor of The Sacred, *a book that presents Indian spirituality and beliefs in the words of the elders.*

I AM OF THE EARTH

I am of the earth
She is my mother
She bore me with pride
She reared me with love
She cradled me each evening
She pushed the wind to make it sing
She built me a house of harmonious colors
She fed me the fruits of her fields
She rewarded me with memories of her smiles
She punished me with the passing of time
And at last, when I long to leave
She will embrace me for eternity.

▼

A NAVAJO CREATION STORY

Creation myths explain how the world came to be and how many features of Indian cultures began. These stories of human creation and the beginnings of culture present the common belief that people are part of the natural world, related to all creations above the earth, on its lands, in its waters, and below the earth. The following Navajo creation myth is based on a legend reported by Washington Matthews in 1897.

CREATION OF FIRST MAN AND FIRST WOMAN

The first people came up through three worlds and settled in the fourth world. They had been driven from each successive world because they had quarreled with one another and committed adultery. In previous worlds they found no other people like themselves, but in the fourth world they found the Kisani or Pueblo people.

The surface of the fourth world was mixed black and white, and the sky was mostly blue and black. There were no sun, no moon, no stars, but there were four great snow-covered peaks on the horizon in each of the cardinal directions.

Late in the autumn they heard in the east the distant sound of a great voice calling. They listened and waited, and soon heard the voice nearer and louder than before. Once more they listened and heard it louder still, very near. A moment later four mysterious beings appeared. These were White Body, god of this world; Blue Body, the sprinkler; Yellow Body; and Black Body, the god of fire.

Using signs but without speaking, the gods tried to instruct the people, but they were not understood. When the gods had gone, the people discussed their mysterious visit and tried without success to figure out the signs. The gods appeared on four days in succession and attempted to communicate through signs, but their efforts came to nothing.

On the fourth day when the other gods departed, Black Body remained behind and spoke to the people in their own language, "You do not seem to understand our signs, so I must tell you what they mean. We want to make people who look more like us. You have bodies like ours, but have the teeth, the feet, and the claws of beasts and insects. The new humans will have hands and feet like ours. Also, you are unclean; you smell bad. We will come back in twelve days. Be clean when we return."

On the morning of the twelfth day the people washed themselves well. Then the women dried their skin with yellow cornmeal, the men with white cornmeal. Soon they heard the distant call, shouted four times, of the approaching gods. When the gods appeared, Blue Body and Black Body each carried a sacred buckskin. White Body carried two ears of corn, one yellow, one white, each covered completely with grains.

The gods laid one buckskin on the ground with the head to the west, and on this they placed the two ears of corn with their tips to the east. Over the corn they spread the other buckskin with its head to the east. Under the white ear they put the feather of a white eagle; under the yellow ear the feather of a yellow eagle. Then they told the people to stand back and allow the wind to enter. Between the skins the white wind blew from the east and the yellow wind from the west. While the wind was blowing, eight of the gods, the Mirage People, came and walked around the objects on

Creation of North Sacred Mountain, by Harrison Begay (Navajo), about 1955.

the ground four times. As they walked the eagle feathers, whose tips protruded from the buckskins, were seen to move. When the Mirage People had finished their walk, the upper buckskin was lifted. The ears of corn had disappeared; a man and a woman lay in their place.

The white ear of corn had become the man, the yellow ear the woman, First Man and First Woman. It was the wind that gave them life, and it is the wind that comes out of our mouths now that gives us life. When this ceases to blow, we die.

The gods had the people build an enclosure of brushwood, and when it was finished, First Man and First Woman went in. The gods told them, "Live together now as husband and wife."

At the end of four days, First Woman bore twins. In four more days she gave birth to a boy and a girl, who grew to maturity in four days and lived with one another as husband and wife. In all, First Man and First Woman had five pairs of twins, and all except the first became couples who had children.

In four days after the last twins were born, the gods came again and took First Man and First Woman away to the eastern mountain, dwelling place of the gods. The couple stayed there for four days, and when they returned, all their children were taken to the eastern mountain for four days. The gods may have taught them the awful secrets of witch-craft. Witches always use masks, and after they returned, they would occasionally put on masks and pray for the good things they needed—abundant rain and abundant crops.

Witches also marry people who are too closely related to them, which is what First Man and First Woman's children had done. After they had been to the eastern mountain, however, the brothers and sisters separated. Keeping their first marriages secret, the brothers now married women of the Mirage People and the sisters married men of the Mirage People. But they never told anyone, even their new families, the mysteries they had learned from the gods. Every four days the women bore children, who grew to maturity in four days, then married, and in their turn had children every four days. In this way many children of First Man and First Woman filled the land with people.

▼

BLACK ELK (OGLALA SIOUX)

Black Elk Speaks, *written by John G. Neihardt, is one of the best-known examples of the "as told to" Indian biographies. Black Elk, an Oglala Sioux warrior and medicine man, told his story in the Sioux language. It was translated into English by his son, Benjamin Black Elk, and then John Neihardt, a non-Indian poet, prepared the manuscript for publication. In this excerpt, Black Elk speaks of his beliefs, his life, his vision, and finally his pain that the flowering tree was withered and the sacred hoop broken in the Battle of Wounded Knee in 1890.*

BLACK ELK SPEAKS

. . . everything an Indian does is in a circle, and that is because the Power of the World always works in circles, and everything tries to be round. In the old days when we were a strong and happy people, all our power came to us from the sacred hoop of the nation, and so long as the hoop was unbroken, the people flourished. The flowering tree was the living center of the hoop, and the circle of the four quarters nourished it. The east gave peace and light, the south gave warmth, the west gave rain, and the north with its cold and mighty wind gave strength and endurance. This knowledge came to us from the outer world with our religion. Everything the Power of the World does is done in a circle. The sky is round, and I have heard that the earth is round like a ball, and so are all the stars. The wind, in its greatest power, whirls. Birds make their nests in circles, for theirs is the same religion as ours. The sun comes forth and goes down again in a circle. The moon does the same, and both are round. Even the seasons form a great circle in their changing, and always come back again to where they were. The life of a man is a circle from childhood to childhood, and so it is in everything where power moves. Our tepees were round like the nests of birds, and these were always set in a circle, the nation's hoop, a nest of many nests, where the Great Spirit meant for us to hatch our children.

▼

PETALESHARO (PAWNEE)

Petalesharo was born about 1797 and died in 1874. He was the principal chief of the Pawnee Nation. In 1821, Petalesharo visited Baltimore, New York, and Philadelphia and attended a New Year's reception at the White House. This speech was delivered at a conference on February 4, 1822. One conference participant was President James Monroe, who had urged Petalesharo to follow the way of peace and be friendly with the people of the United States.

IT IS TOO SOON, MY GREAT FATHER, TO SEND THOSE GOOD MEN AMONG US

My Great Father: I have traveled a great distance to see you—I have seen you and my heart rejoices. I have heard your words—they have entered one ear and shall not escape the other, and I will carry them to my people as pure as they came from your mouth.

My Great Father: I am going to speak the truth. The Great Spirit looks down upon us, and I call Him to witness all that may pass between us on this occasion. If I am here now and have seen your people, your houses, your vessels on the big lake, and a great many wonderful things far beyond my comprehension which appear to have been made by the Great Spirit and placed in your hands, I am indebted to my Father here, who invited me from home, under whose wings I have been protected. Yes, my Great Father, I have traveled with your chief; I have followed him, and trod in his tracks; but there is still another Great Father to whom I am much indebted—it is the Father of us all. Him who made us and placed us on this earth. I feel grateful to the Great Spirit for strengthening my heart for such an undertaking, and for preserving the life which he gave me. The Great Spirit made us all—he made my skin red, and yours white; he placed us on this earth, and intended that we should live differently from each other.

He made the whites to cultivate the earth, and feed on domestic animals; but he made us, red skins, to rove through the uncultivated woods and plains; to feed on wild animals; and to dress with their skins. He also intended that we should go to war—to take scalps—steal horses from and triumph over our enemies—cultivate peace at home, and promote the happiness of each other. I believe there are no people of any colour on this earth who do not believe in the Great Spirit—in rewards, and in punishments. We worship him, but we worship him not as you do. We differ from you in appearance and manners as well as in our customs; and we differ from you in our religion: we have no large houses as you have to worship the Great Spirit in; if we had them today, we should want others tomorrow, for we have not, like you, a fixed habitation—we have no settled home except our villages, where we remain but two moons in twelve. We, like animals, rove through the country, whilst you whites reside between us and heaven; but still, my Great Father, we love the Great Spirit—we acknowledge his supreme power—our peace, our health, and our happiness depend upon him, and our lives belong to him—he made us and he can destroy us.

My Great Father: Some of your good chiefs, as they are called [missionaries], have proposed to send some of their good people among us to change our habits, to make us work and live like the white people. I will not tell a lie—I am going to tell the truth. You love your country—you love your people—you love the manner in which they live, and you think your people brave. I am like you, my Great Father, I love my country—I love my people—I love the manner in which they live, and think myself and warriors brave. Spare me then, Father; let me enjoy my country, and pursue the buffalo, and the beaver, and the other wild animals of our country, and I will trade their skins with your people. I have grown up, and lived thus long without work—I am in hopes you will suffer me to die without it. We have plenty of buffalo, beaver, deer and other wild animals—we have plenty of land, if you will keep your people off of it. My father has a piece on which he lives [Council Bluffs] and we wish him to enjoy it—we have enough without it—but we wish him to live near us to give us good counsel—to keep our ears and eyes open that we may continue to pursue the right road—the road to happiness. He settles all differences between us and the whites, between the red skins themselves—he makes the whites do justice to the red skins, and he makes the red skins do justice to the whites. He saves the effusion of human blood, and restores peace and happiness on the land. You have already sent us a father; it is enough he knows us and we know him—we have confidence in him—we keep our eye constantly upon him, and since we have heard your words, we will listen more attentively to his.

It is too soon, my Great Father, to send those good men among us. We are not starving yet—we wish you to permit us to enjoy the chase until the game of our country is exhausted—until the wild animals become extinct. Let us exhaust our present resources before you make us toil and interrupt our happiness—let me continue to live as I have done, and after I have passed to the Good or Evil Spirit from off the wilderness of my present life, the subsistence of my children may become so precarious as to need and embrace the assistance of those good people. . . .

Here, my Great Father, is a pipe which I present you, as I am accustomed to present pipes to all the red skins in peace with us. It is filled with such tobacco as we were accustomed to smoke before we knew the white people. It is pleasant, and the spontaneous growth of the most remote parts of our country. I know that the robes, leggins, mockasins, bear claws, etc., are of little value to you, but we wish you to have them deposited and preserved in some conspicuous part of your lodge, so that when we are gone and the sod turned over our bones, if our children should visit this place, as we do now, they may see and recognize with pleasure the deposits of their fathers; and reflect on the times that are past.

▼

NAVAJO CEREMONIAL POEM

Repetition is common in Indian ceremonies and literature, serving to focus on and reinforce the theme. Paula Gunn Allen has said that it creates a hypnotic effect where "breath, heartbeat, thought, emotion, and word are one."[5] *In the following poem, as in the selection from the* Night Chant, *repetition brings focus to central beliefs of interdependence and harmony.*

PRAYER TO A DEAD BUCK

In the future that we may continue to hold each other with
    the turquoise hand
Now that you may return to the place from which you came
In the future as time goes on that I may rely on you for food
To the home of the dawn you are starting to return
With the jet hoofs you are starting to return
By means of the zigzag lightning you are starting to return
By the evening twilight your legs are yellow
That way you are starting to return
By the white of dawn your buttocks are white and that way
    you are starting to return
A dark tail is in your tail and that way you are starting to
    return
A haze is in your fur and that way you are starting to return

A growing vegetation is in your ears and that way you are
    starting to return
A mixture of beautiful flowers and water is in your intestines
    and that way you are starting to return
May turquoise be in your liver and abalone shell the parti-
    tion between your heart and intestines
    and that way you are starting to return
May red shell be your lungs and white shell be your wind-
    pipe and that way you are starting to return
May dark wind and straight lightning be your speech
    and that way you are starting to return
There you have returned within the interior of the jet basket
    in the midst of the beautiful flower pollens
Beautifully you have arrived home

Buffalo Hunt, by Nah-Koh-Hist (Cheyenne), about 1876.

Beautifully may you and I both continue to live
From this day may you lead the other game along the trails
    that I may hunt
Because I have obeyed all the restrictions laid down by your
    god in hunting and skinning you
Therefore I ask for this luck that I may continue to have
    good luck in hunting you

▼

JOSEPH BRUCHAC (ABNAKI)

As a contemporary writer, storyteller, and teacher, Joseph Bruchac keeps Indian traditions alive and meaningful today. He is active in writing for young people and their teachers, in assisting novice Indian writers, and in publishing the works of established Indian authors. He has recorded many Indian legends and so made available to a wide audience the great power of traditional storytelling.

THE REMEDIES

Half on the Earth, half in the heart,
the remedies for all the things
which grieve us wait for those who know
the words to use to find them.

Penobscot people used to make
a medicine for cancer from Mayapple
and South American people knew
the quinine cure for malaria
a thousand years ago.

But it is not just in the roots,
the stems, the leaves,
the thousand flowers
that healing lies.
Half of it lives within the words
the healer speaks.

And when the final time has come
for one to leave this Earth
there are no cures,
for Death is only
part of Life, not a disease.

Half on the Earth, half in the heart,
the remedies for all our pains
wait for the songs of healing.

PART TWO

TRADITIONS

Laguna to me is where you go when you're going home. Laguna to me is where people are grounded. Laguna is Feast Day. What I remember about that, one of the first things I ever remember, is leaving Feast with my grandparents and looking out the back window of the car. It was dark and there were fires. Laguna is on a hill and you could see campfires on all the hills around it.... To me, that was the absolute essence of a perfect place to be. That was it.

—*Paula Gunn Allen* [6]

Paula Gunn Allen, a writer from the Laguna Pueblo, speaks of the personal importance of the traditional Laguna Feast Day, the bonfires, and the Pueblo itself. These traditions are at the core of her memories of childhood, and they remain the essence of her being.

Since beliefs are not visible or concrete but are held in our minds, spirits, and hearts, we find ways to show or demonstrate what we believe. These beliefs take form in the traditions that we create and honor. Traditions help us to understand each other, give our lives a shared meaning, and are used to keep beliefs alive and to bind groups together. Without traditions, people feel disconnected, without roots, and often without purpose or meaning in their everyday lives.

Our traditions often have their roots so far back in history that we no longer remember when or why they were created; they have a timeless quality about them, a sense of "this is what we've always done." But traditions aren't always timeless; new holidays and traditions continue to be created to honor people or events who represent our values and beliefs.

Religious ceremonies and rituals are traditions that are central and sacred in Indian life. These ceremonies are often called ritual drama by literary scholars, but to the People, they are simply beautiful spiritual traditions that are fundamental to life.

Maple Sugar Time, by Patrick Desjarlait (Ojibwa/Chippewa), 1946.

Indian cultures have traditional, tribal ways of naming a baby or older person, acknowledging puberty, performing weddings and funerals, showing respect for elders, planting and harvesting crops, praying before and after a hunt, and healing illnesses. Traditions also include celebrations of thanksgiving and a variety of social events.

One example of an Indian tradition common to most North American tribes is the use of tobacco, which is sacred to most tribes, except those from Alaska. Stone pipes dating from as long ago as 2000 B.C. have been unearthed in graves and sacred sites. It is through the sacred pipe and the smoke of the tobacco that prayers are sent and the help of the spirits is enlisted. To be a "Keeper of the Pipe" has a special significance. Smoke from the pipe or the burning of sage, cedar, or sweetgrass is said to purify or cleanse. This ritual is called "smudging." Individuals, groups, rooms, buildings, events, and objects are smudged to cleanse and bless them and to bring the sacred and the spiritual into consciousness. Through these traditions people affirm, "I am Indian."

Stories are one way of keeping both tribal traditions and history alive, and they teach children what is right, wrong, wise, and sacred. They are told from memory and have an intriguing, enduring quality. One of the sacred duties of the elders of the tribes is to hand down the traditions to the younger generations. The best storytellers are highly respected by their people; they were not only entertainers, but also teachers, historians, and guardians of the sacred ceremonies.

When traditional stories are passed down, no one says what the listener is supposed to learn. LaDonna Harris relates how, with each telling of the story, the teller asks, "What did you learn?" Then, one day, many repetitions later and after much conversation, the teller will say to the listener, "Well, I believe you are now a teller of that story!" At that point, the listener has become an owner of that wisdom . . . a teacher.

In the following section on traditions, you will learn about old and new traditions of Indian individuals, families, and tribes, and you will read some of the stories that teach about these traditions.

▼

Legends are said to come from the hearts and souls of Indian people. They vary according to a people's way of life and where they live. Legends tell how special things and places came to be. Raven Hail—a poet, storyteller, musician, editor, and herbalist—tells the story of how the Cherokee rose came to be.

LEGEND OF THE CHEROKEE ROSE

The Old Ones say that long, long ago in the Year of the Big Harvest, the land of the Cherokees was becoming too densely populated and they realized they must spread out into the neighboring lands in order to grow and prosper. The Peace Chief sent out a party of the leading men of the Nation to talk with the neighboring Creeks, who claimed vast areas of land which would be suitable. The Creeks were not as strong as the Cherokees: they had been at war for a long time.

The Cherokees sat in Council with the Creeks to arrange the terms of the exchange of territory. This Council lasted for many days, for there were many amenities to be observed. It is polite to sit in complete silence at the beginning. First the Medicine Man must enact the lengthy Invocation; then the Peace Pipe Ceremony must be performed. The Pipe is passed leisurely around to each member in turn. Some elaborate speeches of greeting and the presentation of gifts must express the good will of the visitors. These must be answered by the hosts. All this must not be hurried, lest it appear that they were eager to get the business over with and go on home. At the end of each day, the Creeks prepared an elaborate feast which was served by the young maidens. The most beautiful maiden of them all was the Daughter of the Chief.

In the ranks of the Cherokee group was Little Hawk, nephew and heir of one of the powerful Red Chiefs. The first night he sat long around the campfire composing a love song. The next afternoon he did not appear at the Council meeting. He was playing the new song on his flute near the lodge of the Chief of the Creeks.

They met in secret and enjoyed the thrill of a forbidden adventure. They gathered wildflowers; they waded barefoot across the stream following after the shrill cry of the blue jay. He told her of the land of his people, where the sun is always shining and the cold winds never blow. He knew that he was expected to choose a wife from the proper Clan of an important Cherokee Village, thus increasing the power and solidarity of the Nation. But the Redbird Spirit of Love pays no heed to the notions of nations, and fluttered at the breast of the young Muskokee maiden, the Daughter of the Chief.

The young lovers finally agreed that when the Council was ended, and his people went on their way, he would come for her. They planned that if he should be detained, she would hide in the thicket at the bend of the river, and he would come for her there.

The Creeks agreed to move back past the banks of the Chattahoochee to allow for the expansion of the Cherokee Nation. Some of the Creek Warriors objected to the trading away of their lands and wanted to fight for it, but the Chief could see that there was no chance of saving the land. He argued that it was better to trade it away than to lose it, along with many lives. So when the Cherokees had left, and the Daughter of the Creek Chief was missing, the Creek Warriors joined in the search for her. Unfortunately, they were the first to find her hiding place.

When the Little Hawk arrived, he found her—dead. He buried her there, and, rejoining his own group, started the long journey homeward. He returned the next Spring and found among the bright green leaves that grew over the mound the tender white petals of the wild rose. He knelt beside it and called it *The Rose of the Cherokee*, for he had claimed her for his own. He carried it back to his home and planted it. But long before the long winter was over he grew eager to see the blossoms again; so he went back to her grave and waited until death came.

The flowers spread throughout the land of the Cherokees and to this day, the Cherokee rose is the first flower to bloom—her eager face opening early in spring to welcome the return of her loved one.

▼

LESLIE MARMON SILKO
(LAGUNA PUEBLO)

Leslie Marmon Silko was born in Albuquerque in 1948 and is best known for her novel Ceremony. *For a time she attended law school but finally decided to turn to writing. Her childhood, rich in the oral tradition of the Laguna and Keres people, has influenced how she views the world and how she writes. She was awarded a coveted MacArthur Foundation grant to complete her latest novel,* Almanac of the Dead.

CEREMONY

I will tell you something about stories,
[he said]
They aren't just entertainment.
Don't be fooled.
They are all we have, you see,
all we have to fight off illness and death.

You don't have anything
if you don't have the stories.

Their evil is mighty
but it can't stand up to our stories.
So they try to destroy the stories
let the stories be confused or forgotten.
They would like that
They would be happy
Because we would be defenseless then.

He rubbed his belly.
I keep them here
[he said]
Here, put your hand on it
See, it is moving.
There is life here
for the people.

And in the belly of this story
the rituals and the ceremony
are still growing.

What She said:
The only cure
I know
is a good ceremony,
that's what she said.

▼

SIMON J. ORTIZ
(ACOMA PUEBLO)

*The trickster is a familiar character in traditional and con-
temporary Indian literature. Animal tricksters include
hare, raven, and coyote. Coyote confuses, infuriates, em-
barrasses, and teaches. Simon Ortiz's book,* Going for the
Rain, *features several poems about Coyote the trickster.*

THE CREATION:
ACCORDING TO COYOTE

"First of all, it's all true."
Coyote, he says this, this way,
humble yourself, motioning and meaning
what he says.

You were born when you came from that body, the earth;
your black head burst from granite,
the ashes cooling
until it began to rain.

Coyote-Koshare, by Harry Fonseca (Maidu), 1981.

It turned muddy then,
and then green and brown things
came without legs.

They looked strange.
Everything was strange.
There was nothing to know then,

Until later, Coyote told me this,
and he was bullshitting probably,
two sons were born,
Uyuyayeh and Masawe.

They were young then
and then later on they were older.
And then the people were wondering
what was above.
They had heard rumors.

But, you know, Coyote,
he was mainly bragging
when he said (I think),
"My brothers, the Twins then said,
'Let's lead these poor creatures and save them.' "

And later on, they came to light
after many exciting
and colorful and tragic things
having to do with adventure,
and this is the life, all these, all these.

My uncle told me all this, that time.
Coyote told me too, but you know
how he is, always talking to the gods,
and mountains, the stone all around

And you know, I believe him.

▼

LUTHER STANDING BEAR
(SIOUX)

*Although Luther Standing Bear (Plenty Kill) called himself
an Oglala Sioux, one of the bands of the Teton Sioux, it is
believed that he was probably a Brule Sioux. He was given*

the name Luther Standing Bear at the Carlisle Indian School in Pennslyvania, where he was a member of its first class. A victim of the extraordinary efforts to assimilate the Indian into the Anglo-European culture, he wrote to inform whites of the value of Indian life and traditions. In his preface to Land of the Spotted Eagle, *one of his four books, he wrote: "White men seem to have difficulty in realizing that people who live differently from themselves still might be traveling the upward and progressive road of life." This is a chapter about religion from that book.*

INDIAN WISDOM

The Lakota loved the sun and earth, but he worshiped only Wakan Tanka, or Big Holy, who was the Maker of all things of earth, sky, and water. Wakan Tanka breathed life and motion into all things, both visible and invisible. He was over all, through all, and in all, and great as was the sun and good as was the earth, the greatness and goodness of the Big Holy were not surpassed. The Lakota could look at nothing without at the same time looking at Wakan Tanka, and he could not, if he wished, evade His presence, for it pervaded all things and filled all space. All the mysteries of birth, life, and death; all the wonders of lightning, thunder, wind, and rain were but the evidence of His everlasting and encompassing power. . . .

For the most part the Lakota was a silent and solitary worshiper, though in many of the religious rituals prayer was offered in speech and song. Prayer, however, was not so much a matter of supplication as it was of thanksgiving, and favorite words for beginning a prayer were, *Tunka sila le iyahpe ya yo*, which translated says, "Father, receive my offering."

Sometimes a silent family prayer was held. The father or head of the family smoked a few puffs while the mother and children sat in respectful silence until he had finished. If a number of people had gathered for devotion, they usually seated themselves in a circle while some brave performed the pipe ceremony. The pipe was passed around the circle, each male member of the group taking a puff; or, if a brave did not care to smoke, he touched the tip with his lips or laid his hands gently and respectfully upon the stem. Still another way of conducting the devotion was to blow the smoke in the mouth into cupped hands, then rub the hands over head and arms as if pouring water over the body. Again, the sacred or offering pole might inspire one to prayer. A brave, usually a father or head of a family, would get his pipe and stand beside the pole. He would first give the pipe ceremony, then sing his song of prayer, everyone hearing his voice joining him. Even children at play stopped until the prayer song was over.

Sometimes a two or three days' ceremony of *Waunyapi* was held. A sacred pole was placed either inside the tipi, between the fire and the door, or just outside the door, to which anyone in the village wishing to join the ceremony of giving thanks tied a bundle of food or other gifts as expression of gratefulness. Sometimes these bundles were so many that they were tied to all the poles, and gifts were taken to some solitary place and there dedicated to Wakan Tanka.

An object of special veneration, for which a shrine was

erected in a tipi only for that purpose, was the white buffalo hide. Because of their rarity these hides were never made into garments but were kept for ceremonial purposes only. It was said by hunters that these white or albino buffaloes, which were nearly always female, could far outrun the dark animals. Shrines were also erected in memory and respect of the dead in which a strand of hair, typifying the living spirit of the buried body, was the object of adoration. The hair of the loved one was wrapped in a bundle the covering of which was beautified with paintings, porcupine-quillwork or design, and then hung on a tripod which was painted red. The tripod was very often placed just outside the tipi door where it was easily watched and protected from rain. At other times a tipi was especially erected to house the shrine to which gift offerings were taken and tied to the poles to be distributed to the people on a day set for memorial services. Anyone entering the tipi of the sacred bundle was quiet and respectful, and should the camp move, the tipi and the tripod were the first to be set up.

Our altars were built on the ground and were altars of thankfulness and gratefulness. They were made of sacred earth and placed upon the holiest of all places—the lap of Mother Earth. The altar was built in a square mound, each side being from a foot and a half to three feet in length, according to the size of the ceremonial space. One half of the altar was painted green to symbolize the earth and the other half painted yellow to symbolize the sky. At each corner of the altar was placed an upright stick and to the top of each stick was tied a small buckskin bag holding the sacred tobacco. The buffalo skull was placed in the center of the mound on the heap of earth. Close to the altar and against a rack stood the pipe, without which no altar was complete.

Altars were built whenever circumstances called for them and at no set time nor special place; and any individual prompted by the spirit of devotion could erect one. They were built for all religious ceremonies, such as the Confirmation and Sun Dances and sometimes for the sick. If a sick one was being treated in the sweat-house, then the altar was placed opposite the opening of the sweat-lodge. When the ceremonies were over and the altars were no longer needed, the earth was scattered.

Wild sage, which was a symbol of cleanliness and purity, was a necessary part of every sacred ceremony. It was brought to the Lakotas in a vision, and the Sun Dancers wrapped it around their ankles and wrists. Small sprigs of it were tied to the eagle-bone whistles next to the mouthpiece, and when the dancers began to feel thirst they chewed a bit of it. Those who went into the sweat-lodge either because of illness or for purification rubbed their bodies with this sweet-smelling shrub, and a tea brewed from its leaves relieved headache and indigestion. Every altar was adorned with it and, according to legend, the floor of the holy tipi in which the Sun Woman sat for ten days and nights was carpeted with its boughs.

But of all things held sacred and reverent, the pipe stood supreme in the minds of the Lakota people. It, too, was brought untold years ago in the decalogue of the Sun Woman to be held forever sacred and its mandates to be unquestioningly obeyed. The pipe was a tangible, visible link that joined man to Wakan Tanka and every puff of smoke that ascended in prayer unfailingly reached His presence. With it faith was upheld, ceremony sanctified, and the being consecrated. All the meanings of moral duty, ethics, religious and spiritual conceptions were symbolized in the pipe. It signified brotherhood, peace, and the perfection of Wakan Tanka, and to the Lakota the pipe stood for that which the Bible, Church, State, and Flag, all combined, represented in the mind of the white man. Without the pipe no altar was complete and no ceremony effective. It was used in council, all religious dance ceremonials, in consecrating a life to the labor and service of band members, smoked by the scout to bind his word to truth, in salute and reverence to the rising sun, and by the man who mourned for the death of a loved one that it might dispatch grief and bring peace and solace.

To own a pipe was to own a priceless possession and in many tipis there was one carefully cared for—not the finely decorated pipe, for that was usually cared for by a chief or one of the peacemakers, but a simple pipe whom any reverent one might own. Those who did not have a pipe in their tipi were always welcome to go to a tipi where there was one and there smoke and commune with Wakan Tanka, but it was an article that was never borrowed. Smoking was the Indian Angelus, and whenever its smoke ascended, men, women, and children acknowledged the sacred presence of their Big Holy.

Peace was the pipe's greatest significance—a peace never more deeply and thoughtfully conceived by any man or society of men. Of all symbols that ever inspired men the

Pipe of Peace was the strongest. Standards, typifying the ideals of societies, have been worshiped and followed, but none have exerted so great an influence toward peace and brotherhood as this symbol. Its motto was *Wolakota wa yaka cola*, "Peace without slavery!" Not another standard but has been desecrated by war; not another but has led men into unholy conflict and there *are none to keep them from war except the Pipe of Peace.* If this sacred symbol was taken to Lakota warriors in the thickest of battle, they would at once obey its mandate and retire. To disobey was to suffer personal disaster and it is Lakota history that no warrior ever disobeyed without at last dying an ignominious death.

Peace—that ideal which man may sometime reach—was symbolized in the Pipe of Peace and, under the society of the pipe, or codes symbolized by the pipe, native man made the most effectual effort at arriving at peace ever made on this continent. It was but a start, perhaps, but its strength lay in the fact that under the Great Peace, women had begun the necessary foundational work for the elimination of war by raising sons who could participate only in pursuits of peace. War was excluded from the existence of a certain portion of the male population and in this move the Indian mother pointed the way and the only road to the realization of peace between all men. The acceptance of a kinship with other orders of life was the first step toward humanization and the second step was the dedication of sons to peace, the spiritual value of which is incalculable; and not until the women of the land come back to the forsaken road, emulate the Indian mother, and again raise sons for peace will there be any substantial move toward "peace on earth and good-will toward men."

▼

A TETON SIOUX SONG

The more traditional songs of the Teton Sioux tend to deal with war, hunting, and sacred ceremonies, while their modern songs are love songs or songs that are social in nature.

SONG CONCERNING A
MESSAGE FROM WASHINGTON

The great grandfather (the President)
has said,
so they report,
"Dakotas,
be citizens,"
he said,
so they report.
But
it will be impossible for me.
The Dakota (ways)
them
I love,
I said.
Therefore
I have helped (to keep the old ways).

▼

KIOWA WIND SONGS

Wind Songs are a special kind of song sung by someone who is thinking of a beloved warrior who is far from home or by a lonely warrior remembering his home and loved ones. They

are called Wind Songs because they tell of loneliness and
sadness and are reminiscent of the vast sweeps of prairies
where the only sound is that of the wind.

MAIDEN'S SONG

Idlers and cowards are here at home now,
Whenever they wish, they see their loved ones.
O idlers and cowards are here at home now,
O idlers and cowards are here at home now,
But the young man I love has gone to war, far away.
Weary, lonely, he longs for me.

YOUNG WARRIOR'S SONG

You young men sitting there,
You have wealth and parents, relatives, friends.
But me, I am a poor and lonely boy.
I will remain here and go on another expedition,
I know how to sleep and eat on the prairie
        away from home.
This kind of life makes me happy and content.

LONELY MAIDEN'S SONG

When I see your parents and family,
My heart is filled with joy;
It is as if I saw you in person.
Why do you act hard to get?
I heard that you are not coming home,
But will leave again for another journey.

NORA NARANJO-MORSE
(TEWA-SANTA CLARA PUEBLO)

In this poem, Nora Naranjo-Morse speaks not only of traditions but of maintaining balance and harmony through change. The importance of the family and the wisdom of elders are perhaps the strongest of Indian traditions.

TA

I asked about success
    how was I to measure it,
    struggling in
    two worlds,
        between Pueblo tradition
        and modern values.
    Keeping on course,
        a balance
        of who I am
            and wish to become.
Ta took his time answering.
    I thought maybe
        he hadn't heard,
        or worse,
        not listened.
    Waiting
        I noticed,
        how time
        had tailored my father

Mother's Prayer, by Archie Blackowl (Southern Cheyenne), 1974.

                    into an old man
                    wrinkled
                              and halting.
        Finally,
                    with clear
                    thoughtful words,
                    my father spoke:
                    "Navi a yu,
                    hi wu na mang,
                    uvi aa yaa,
                    uvi seng,
                    da hihchan po o.
                    Navi a yu,

hi wodi kwee un muu,
oe to jan be,
hi wo na mang,
sa wo na mang."
"My daughter,
it is going well,
your children,
your husband,
are happy.
My daughter,
you are a good woman,
listen,
it is going well,
it goes in beauty."
Simple
        words,
                reminding me,
                success
                is not only
                respecting tradition
                or balancing modern values.
                It is the appreciation
                of life's basic gifts,
                weaving
                into the whole
                of who you are
                and who you can become.
Ta sat under the Elm,
        drifting to sleep
                his hand in mine.

▼

FOUR GUNS (OGLALA SIOUX)

This was a speech delivered by Four Guns in 1891, after a dinner given by anthropologist Clark Wissler. After-dinner speaking was unfamiliar to him and, as you will read, it also made little sense to him, a man to whom words were sacred and the traditions of his people dear.

THE INDIAN NEEDS NO WRITING

I have visited the Great Father in Washington. I have attended dinners among white people. Their ways are not our ways. We eat in silence, quietly smoke a pipe and depart. Thus is our host honored.

This is not the way of the white man. After his food has been eaten, one is expected to say foolish things. Here the host feels honored. Many of the white man's ways are past understanding, but now that we have eaten at the white man's table, it is fitting that we honor our host according to the ways of his people.

Our host has filled many notebooks with the sayings of our fathers as they came down to us. This is the way of his people; they set great store upon writing; always there is a paper.

But we have learned that though there are many papers in Washington upon which are written promises to pay us for our lands, no white man seems to remember them.

However, we know our host will not forget what he has written down, and we hope that the white people will read it.

But we are puzzled as to what useful service all this writing serves. Whenever white people come together, there is writing. When we go to buy some sugar or tea, we see the white trader busy writing in a book. Even the white doctor as he sits beside his patient, writes on a piece of paper.

The white people must think paper has some mysterious power to help them on in the world.

The Indian needs no writing. Words that are true sink deep into his heart where they remain. He never forgets them. On the other hand, if the white man loses his paper, he is helpless.

I once heard one of their preachers say that no white man was admitted to heaven, unless there were writings about him in a great book.

PART THREE

CHANGE

The winds of change have blown in Indian Country for thousands of years, but until the last five hundred years, change was an ordinary response to the seasons and the natural world. During the last five hundred years, change has been imposed on Native people by outside forces. And this change came too fast and without warning or support for appropriate responses.

—Karen Harvey and Lisa Harjo [7]

Change is inevitable. In fact, those things that do not change are stagnant, dormant, static, dying. What makes change so different and so painful for Indian people is that the change in their lives was imposed by outside forces and frequently had devastating results.

Indians have been decimated by European diseases, the United States cavalry, missionaries, prejudice, discrimination, and governmental policies. Their lands were taken from them, their homes relocated, their children wrenched from them, their means of survival destroyed, their religions suppressed, and their pride and dignity shattered.

Desperately poor reservations, although home to Indian people, are generally located on lands that were rejected by settlers. Unemployment and poverty are rampant, housing is shabby and unsanitary, schooling opportunities are dismal, and health care difficult to obtain. To get enough money to live on, some tribal members have been forced to plunder natural resources or store garbage or nuclear waste on their sacred lands. Others have moved to the cities.

For urban Indians, adjusting to living in large metropolitan areas with the dominant American culture has been an overwhelming challenge. They face serious problems they cannot handle. Frequently they experience difficulty finding jobs, adjusting to an unfamiliar environment, and locating health care. Because of the allure of the city and its promised opportunities, many of those who move from the reservation to the city expect a good job and a decent

The Long Cold Wait, by Alfred Youngman (Cree), 1968.

standard of living. What they experience instead is prejudice, unemployment, poverty, and ill health.

Both on and off reservations, Indians have been devastated by ill health. Heart disease, diabetes, cancer, alcoholism, and accidents are the major killers of American Indians. Their life expectancy is much shorter than that of other Americans. Disease and dysfunction have too frequently become a part of daily life. Forced removal from ancient homesites has caused Native people to accept new foods and customs that have had ill effects on their lives.

Alcoholism is a disease that affects many Indian people. While the obvious reason for their drinking may be depression, poverty, and hopelessness, it is likely that they are also born with an intolerance for alcohol. They seem to have a different reaction to alcohol than other people, and over the years have developed a high rate of alcoholism. Alcoholism has destroyed many lives. Women who drink during their pregnancies may damage their babies irreversibly. These babies born with Fetal Alcohol Syndrome have physical defects and damage to their thinking and problem-solving abilities. Alcohol is related to the high incidence of suicide among Indians, particularly the young, whose experiences with the world have often been unfriendly and filled with extreme social stress and disruption. They feel that they have few, if any, alternatives, and they do not believe that they can determine their future.

Other changes seem less tragic. Technology has enabled people to travel and so expand their tribal experience to knowledge of other worlds and lifeways. And education has trained Indian physicians, attorneys, teachers, artists, and political leaders, most of whom live in two cultures. Yet this change is a mixed blessing, for often these bicultural leaders do not feel completely comfortable in either world.

The literature written by American Indian people often reflects the rage, hopelessness, and alienation that have resulted from such profound change. This is particularly true of contemporary writing, which often expresses a wrenching bitterness or anger. Memory is long, and the pain of early, unwanted change and adaptation remain in the consciousness of many Indian people. This literature of change sounds harsh at times, but it is one of the genuine voices of the People.

▼

LIZ SOHAPPY BAHE
(PALOUSE)

Omnama Cheshuts (Stopping On A Hill And Looking Down), or Liz Sohappy Bahe, was born in 1947 in the state of Washington. She spent her childhood in the Northwest but attended high school at the Institute of American Indian Arts in Santa Fe, New Mexico. She returned to the Institute later to continue her study of poetry.

PRINTED WORDS

I stared at the printed words
hazed, blurred, they became grey.
I trailed down the page
to a picture shouting what I read.

I thought about my people
up North—
far from here.
My land, the hot dry basin,
the pine on the mountain ranges
and the snowcapped peaks.

I thought of the killing word;
Civilization.
The steel buildings stabbing the earth,
stabbing old religions now buried on the hilltop,
to have their tears drip black
from Industry's ash clouds.

I thought of the unseen tears
in eyes watching our valley
gashed by plows,
proud trees uprooted, dragged aside,
giving way to smothering tar roads.
And river veins pumped away
never knowing the path to the Columbia River.

I glanced at the blurring printed words
and felt an ancient anger swell,
bubble like a volcano in birth,
anger blackening the printed words
about your land being only a swamp
useless to Civilization.

I saw in a flash
the unknowing eyes of the Everglades—
alligators, egrets, water turkeys, ibises.
Animals I've never seen, never known
except from sadness that their fate lies
in printed words.

The words about the Everglades—
moist, mysterious, very much a land—
useless.
Words forgetting the animal people,
the Seminole, the Miccosukie,
who are standing in the way of the thing called
Civilization.

▼

N O R A   N A R A N J O - M O R S E
(T E W A - S A N T A   C L A R A   P U E B L O)

Nora Naranjo-Morse is both a writer and a potter. In the traditional manner, she gathers her own clay near her home in Espanola, New Mexico. In the contemporary market of San Ildefonso, she sells her work. Her pottery has been exhibited in galleries around the country, and she has published several volumes of poetry. In this poem she writes about the juxtaposition of old and new, and she also uses one form of expression to write about another.

TRADITION AND CHANGE

My mission was to sell pottery from booth 109,
    so early that morning I drove to San Ildefonso.
I expected this market of arts and crafts to be full,
    A full day in many ways.
    Hundreds of steel-framed booths
    filled the center of the pueblo.
    Cars streamed in at a steady pace,
    while Summer's heat became relentless.
    Oh yes, and there were people, all kinds, from every-
        where,
    looking to buy, with spend in their eyes,
    maybe for pottery.
        I hoped so.
    "Too expensive, Myrtle," I heard a man say to his
        wife,
    as she reached for one of my clay forms,

Mama and Papa Have the Going Home Shiprock Blues,
by T. C. Cannon (Caddo-Kiowa), about 1966.

his words pressing her onward to the next booth.
If it was jewelry they were looking for, this was the
     place.
Everything, from finely crafted turquoise inlaid
     bracelets
to Mickey Mouse earring set in mother of pearl,
his nose in jet, and those shorts of Mickey's
painted in coral stone.
The Summer's temperature rose as a loudspeaker
     blared continuous news of a disco dance
     being held that evening in another pueblo.
     Warning visitors to stay off the kiva steps,
     and reminding us that Navajo tacos were being sold
     at any one of the eight refreshment stands
     along the outer wall of the village.
     A candidate for governor hurried by,
     shaking hands almost desperately
     with anyone who looked of voting age.
It was at that moment I turned away, trying to shake off
     this state I had entered.
     You know, that state of mind that displaces you
     for just a second.
     Oh yes,
     oh yes, this is San Ildefonso Pueblo in the 90's.
All this made me wonder where our people were headed,
     what our ancestors would think about a Navajo Taco
     going for $3.75.
     I thought about changes affecting our tradition,
         change and tradition,
         on this hot full day.

▼

N. SCOTT MOMADAY (KIOWA)

In this excerpt from his award-winning novel, House Made of Dawn, *Scott Momaday describes the conflict and struggle of a returning Indian soldier who is now battling to survive in an urban environment.*

HOUSE MADE OF DAWN

It was kind of hard for him, you know, getting used to everything. We had to get down there [to the factory] pretty early and put in a day's work. And then at night we would go down to Henry's place and fool around. We would get drunk and have a good time. There were always some girls down there, and on paydays we acted pretty big.

But he was unlucky. Everything went along all right for about two months, I guess. And it would have gone all right after that, too, if they had just let him alone. Maybe . . . you never know about a guy like that; but they wouldn't let him alone. The parole officer, and welfare, and the Relocation people kept coming around, you know, and they were always after him about something. They wanted to know how he was doing, had he been staying out of trouble and all. I guess that got on his nerves after a while, especially the business about drinking and running around. They were always *warning* him, you know? Telling him how he had to stay out of trouble, or else he was going to wind up in prison again. I guess he had to think about that all the time, because they wouldn't let him forget it.

Sometimes they talked to me about him, too, and I said he was getting along all right. But he wasn't. And I could see why, but I didn't know how to tell them about it. They wouldn't have understood anyway. You have to get used to everything, you know; it's like starting out someplace where you've never been before, and you don't know where you're going or why or when you have to get there, and everybody's looking at you, waiting for you, wondering why you don't hurry up.

And they can't help you because you don't know how to talk to them. They have a lot of *words,* and you know they mean something, but you don't know what, and your own words are no good because they're not the same; they're different, and they're the only words you've got. Everything is different, and you don't know how to get used to it. You see the way it is, how everything is going on without you, and you start to worry about it. You wonder how you can get yourself into the swing of it, you know? And you don't know how, but you've got to do it because there's nothing else. And you want to do it, because you can see how good it is. It's better than anything you've ever had; it's money and clothes and having plans and going someplace fast. You can see what it's like, but you don't know how to get into it; there's too much of it and it's all around you and you can't get hold of it because it's going on too fast.

You have to get used to it first, and it's hard. You've got to be left alone. You've got to put a lot of things out of your mind, or you're going to get all mixed up. You've got to take it easy and get drunk once in a while and just forget about who you are. It's hard, and you want to give up. You think about getting out and going home. You want to think that

Indian in a Void, by Jack Malotte (Washo/Shoshone), 1981.

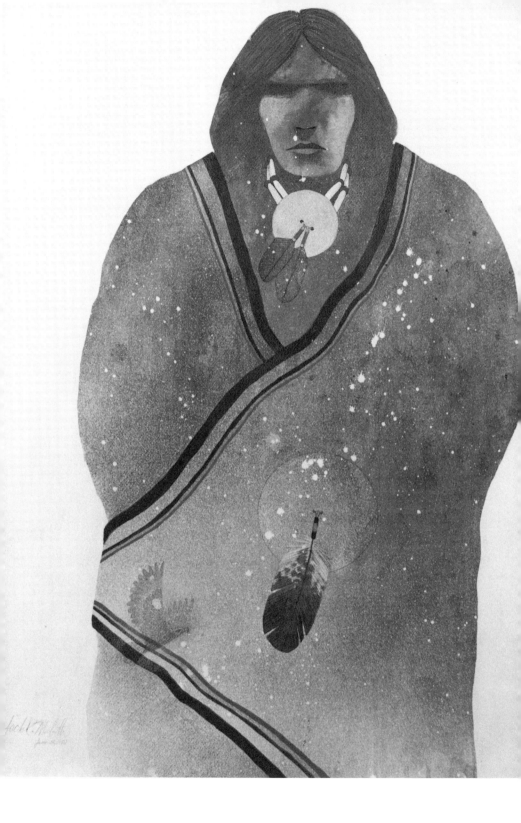

you belong someplace, I guess. You go up there on the hill and you hear the singing and the talk and you think about going home. But the next day you know it's no use; you know that if you went home there would be nothing there, just the empty land and a lot of old people, going no-place and dying off. And you've got to forget about that, too. Well, they were always coming around and warning him. They wouldn't let him alone, and pretty soon I could see that he was getting all mixed up.

▼

MICHAEL DORRIS (MODOC)

Michael Dorris left his position as professor of anthropology and Native American studies to devote his time to writing. His marvelous story of the lives of three women—daughter, mother, and grandmother—deals with complex change woven through time and culture. This particular episode is told in the daughter Rayona's voice and tells of betrayal and survival . . . a familiar story throughout Indian country.

A YELLOW RAFT IN BLUE WATER

For sure, there's no avoiding I am going to fall into Father Tom's clutch. I know he's finally taken a bead on me the day he comes to Aunt Ida's and asks me to be his special assistant at the Mission.

"I really need you, Rayona," he says with a big wet smile. He must count me for at least two of those three-hundred-day indulgences each Beatitude is worth. I recognize all the signs. People have taken me under their wings before.

"I don't know how," I tell him, but he says I can learn, he'll teach me.

I admit I give in without a fight. Father Tom is the last one on the reservation I want to know, but he's the only one who wants to know me. And he needs me more than he thinks.

"I hear you speak your native tongue, Rayona," he says one day after I've arranged the altar for his morning Mass.

Why do they always call it that, "native tongue"?

"My mom is from here." I state a fact he has to know already. "She talked it at home. I can understand it okay."

"*I smell like dogshit!* " Father Tom booms out at me in Indian. The church echoes with his voice. I've heard him say this before. Foxy told Annabelle, who couldn't believe her ears that such a hilarious thing had happened, that when Vance Windyboy, on the Tribal Council, found out Father Tom wanted to learn the language, he gave him some private lessons.

"You shouldn't say that," I say. "Vance is pulling your leg."

Father Tom's face sags. He looks like some kid who just dropped his Popsicle in the dirt. "What does it mean?" he demands, but I shake my head.

"Just say *hello*," I tell him, giving him the ordinary word, "if you have to say something."

Hello doesn't sound halfway as interesting as *I smell like dogshit* to Father Tom's ear. He looks at me and doesn't trust me one bit.

"Ask Father Hurlburt," I suggest, but I can tell from Father Tom's expression that this is not the way he wants to go.

"I guess I'm just no good at languages," he says.

However, from then on, he checks most things with me

before he leaps, and I get pretty well used to having him around. Sometimes he makes me so nervous I want to run from him. But there's no place to go. And sometimes he's all right, kind of familiar. He comes for me two or three times a week. He asks how I am. He talks to me as if I have sense. He reminds me of social workers back in Seattle, and with them I know the questions and the answers I'm supposed to give.

I become the one loyal member of the God Squad, and some meetings it's just him and me and too much Kool-Aid. Each get-together is supposed to have a theme, but no matter what's scheduled, Father Tom finds a way to talk about sex, which he calls "The Wonders of the Human Body." This is a subject about which I have great curiosity but little know-how. People I've known, kids my age, have gotten mixed up in it already and it seems to change them for the worse. Plus, Mom swears off of it for weeks at a time. But I can't help thinking that, if I had the opportunity and knew all the facts in advance, I could keep the situation under control.

It's clear that Father Tom is no expert himself, at least as far as girls are concerned, since all his examples have to do with boys.

"At the age of fourteen or fifteen," he tells me one day as we drive back up the hill to Aunt Ida's, "boys begin to have dreams."

This does not strike me as all that amazing.

"Do you ever have them?" he asks, blushing but trying to act as though it's the most innocent question in the world.

At first I think he means medicine dreams, which I have read about and which the old folks say are supposed to come at about my age, at least to boys. They're the kind of dreams that tell you about who you are and what you're supposed to be. Vision quests. I am interested that Father Tom believes in them too.

"Not yet," I say. "They never write about girls getting them. But I dreamed of a bear once two years ago. Do you think that means something?"

We've stopped at Aunt Ida's house, and the truck engine is idling. Father Tom gives me a crosseyed look.

"No, *dreams*," he says. "About the Wonders of the Human Body."

He means sex. His skin turns splotchy red and he looks like one of those mooseheads that are stuffed with a grin on their face. "Have you had that kind of dream?"

I am so surprised by his question that I say yes, which is dumb to do because he wants to hear what they were about.

"I will understand," he says. "No matter what they are."

"It's bad luck to tell your dreams," I warn him, but he won't stop.

"I can help you, Rayona. You need the guidance of an older friend. You have reached the age of puberty and are turning into a young lady."

I get out of the truck and don't look back. His words lasso me.

"An attractive young lady."

It's the first time since the day Mom split that I think I'm really going to lose it. Something rises inside me so hard I think it will lift me off the ground and ram me into the side of the house. I start to turn and face the truck. But it's in reverse. I hear it back down the hill whining and clanking over the rough ground. When it hits bottom, before it heads toward the Mission, there is a pause. I know without looking that it's out of sight, that Father Tom can't see me standing here, can't know I'm caught by his words. The horn sounds once, twice, more times in a kind of beat. The tires catch, the truck moves off, and for an instant there is a hole of quiet, a pocket of air without any noise, before the call of radios and televisions and bees and wind rushes in to fill my ears.

▼

JACK FORBES
(POWHATAN-DELAWARE)

Jack Forbes was born in California and continues to live there. He has spoken of his tribal heritage as part of the Indian trail along which his people have been slowly driven from the East Coast to the West. Forbes has achieved prominence as an educator, specializing in multicultural education.

His recent work has included writing for journals and newspapers as well as fiction.

ONLY APPROVED INDIANS CAN PLAY: MADE IN USA

The All-Indian Basketball Tournament was in its second day. Excitement was pretty high, because a lot of the teams were very good or at least eager and hungry to win. Quite a few people had come to watch, mostly Indians. Many were relatives or friends of the players. A lot of people were betting money and tension was pretty great.

A team from the Tucson Inter-Tribal House was set to play

against a group from the Great Lakes region. The Tucson players were mostly very dark young men with long black hair. A few had little goatee beards or mustaches though, and one of the Great Lakes fans had started a rumor that they were really Chicanos. This was a big issue since the Indian Sports League had a rule that all players had to be of one-quarter or more Indian blood and that they had to have their BIA roll numbers available if challenged.

And so a big argument started. One of the biggest, darkest Indians on the Tucson team had been singled out as a Chicano, and the crowd wanted him thrown out. The Great Lakes players, most of whom were pretty light, refused to start. They all had their BIA identification cards, encased in plastic. This proved that they were all real Indians, even a blonde-haired guy. He was really only about one-sixteenth but the BIA rolls had been changed for his tribe so legally he was one-fourth. There was no question about the Great Lakes team. They were all land-based, federally-recognized Indians, although living in a big midwestern city, and they had their cards to prove it.

Anyway, the big, dark Tucson Indian turned out to be a Papago. He didn't have a BIA card but he could talk Papago so they let him alone for the time being. Then they turned towards a lean, very Indian-looking guy who had a pretty big goatee. He seemed to have a Spanish accent, so they demanded to see his card.

Well, he didn't have one either. He said he was a full-blood Tarahumara Indian and he could also speak his language. None of the Great Lakes Indians could talk their languages so they said that was no proof of anything, that you had to have a BIA roll number.

The Tarahumara man was getting pretty angry by then. He said his father and uncle had been killed by the whites in Mexico and that he did not expect to be treated with prejudice by other Indians.

But all that did no good. Someone demanded to know if he had a reservation and if his tribe was recognized. He replied that his people lived high up in the mountains and that they were still resisting the Mexicanos, that the government was trying to steal their land.

"What state do your people live in," they wanted to know. When he said that his people lived free, outside of the control of any state, they only shook their fists at him. "You're not an official Indian. All official Indians are under the white man's rule now. We all have a number given to us, to show that we are recognized."

Well, it all came to an end when someone shouted that "Tarahumaras don't exist. They're not listed in the BIA dictionary." Another fan yelled, "He's a Mexican. He can't play. This tournament is only for Indians."

The officials of the tournament had been huddling together. One blew his whistle and an anouncement was made. "The Tucson team is disqualified. One of its members is a Yaqui. One is a Tarahumara. The rest are Papagos. None of them have BIA enrollment cards. They are not Indians within the meaning of the laws of the government of the United States. The Great Lakes team is declared the winner by default."

A tremendous roar of applause swept through the stands. A white BIA official wiped the tears from his eyes and said to a companion, "God Bless America. I think we've won."

▼

RAYNA GREEN (CHEROKEE)

In the introduction to her book, That's What She Said, *Rayna Green speaks of the Indian women who have always told the stories in Indian Country—in clay, fiber, pictures, and words on winter evenings around the fires. She talks about how some things change and other things remain the same. It is the form that changes, she says, not the spirit. This puts change within the context of development, not disaster. Change is linked to survival rather than to destruction.*

THAT'S WHAT SHE SAID

The clay shapers, fiber twisters, picture makers, and storytellers—the ones who said what was and what will be—they've always been important in Indian Country. Whether it comes directly from the storyteller's mouth and she writes it down or someone writes it for her, the story has to be told. Sometimes she hears or dreams something and makes a story out of it. That's the way it often happens. Before European writing, there were voices to sing and speak, dances to make real the stories that the People told or to honor the retelling anew. There were hands that talked and drew and shaped. Some tales could be told with one or two small marks—because the artist knew how to put them together so that those who saw would be reminded of where they came from just from seeing the marks. Others would take eight nights to sing the words so that someone could be healed and the others could remember. And others might get the story as they watched the women weave it into

War Dance Gathering Scene, by Earnest Spybuck (Shawnee), early 1900s.

the rug. They'd have to remember what their duties were toward the People because the rug told them every time they looked at it. Whichever way it was, the story got told, and it gets told now. The old ways of speaking aren't gone. They've changed, of course. There has always been change; there are always new ways to remember. The same people still give shape to mass, color to substance, music to ideas, and words to feelings. Not everyone knows how to do these things, but everyone sees or hears and touches, and some have the special gift to say the right words. They keep them even when no one asked to hear them—even when the white eyes came and asked only the men what they knew.

▼

EMERSON   BLACKHORSE   MITCHELL
(NAVAJO)

Miracle Hill, published in 1967, was written by a young
Navajo boy as an assignment in a creative writing class at
the Institute of American Indian Arts. The assignment for
the duration of the class was to "Write the story of your life
from the time you were born until you are thirty years old."
After initial attempts to "correct" his work, his teacher, Mrs.
Allen, allowed his work to flow into the unique and simple
story of a boy growing up in and between two different
cultures. His teacher and "co-author" of the book later
helped him fill in some of the gaps in the narrative so that it
became what he wanted it to be. The book has a very special
quality that allows us to experience and understand in a
new way what it was like to be a Navajo boy learning about
the white man's world.

MIRACLE HILL

Then, it was Monday when the school began to roll. First
three days of the week, it was orientation in case someone
newcomer might be interested in different fields.

. . . Broneco this time meeting a new teacher before a
desk in the color of gray. "I'm Mrs. Terry Allen and I teach
Creative Writing," she said.

Broneco this time shook hands this teacher and seated
himself before her. "My name is Broneco. Glad to meet you,
Mrs. . . ?"

"Allen," she said, since Broneco has forgotten already.

Broneco then asked a few question which she answered in a few words. Broneco excited him deeply to his satisfaction.

"It's been a long time I have waited for this kind of work. At last, I have found the choice of my own to dream as I please," Broneco thought. "To put the past history in writing so it will always be remembered someday!" Yes, he will major in writing.

. . . A week has gone by tediously as the hours of the day stretched into long moments of time. The endless hours come to Friday. Broneco, in Creative Writing class, sat before the long table, facing the yonder wash packed with adobe villages. Not knowing what to write about or how to start off a story.

Since it was in the afternoon, the sun glitter its ray through the classroom window, made the students in the large square room yawning and closing their eyes fallen asleep.

All of a sudden, a cool summer air blew gently across Broneco's face which half wake him. Mrs. Allen, the writing teacher, let out of her soft pink hands a seed pod of milkweed.

Whirling in circles above the students' head it drifted. Then landing atop the long table it skid, then walking, prancing, Broneco's eyes rolled, following the furry seed dancing before him. Though as someone ice skating in a ballet form of presentation it whirl, spinning, and then stopping.

In a sudden emotion, Broneco's pencil begin to wiggle in jerks. He begin writing his experience in writing a free verse poem.

Mrs. Allen, seated in front of the long table, smiled then took off her eye glass. She paused a minute. "That's it. You doing fine," she said, resuming her daily work, checking and marking papers which was piled high in front of her.

Broneco didn't know he has been thinking and attracted to the seed. He wrote his first poem.

The long boring hours seemed short. Broneco knew it was after school. Smiling, he handed his paper to Mrs. Allen, ready to be graded.

"Broneco, you wrote a poem," she said, adding, "This is good."

"I'm glad you liked it," replied Broneco, leaving the room.

"A poem, yes, It's a poem," thought Broneco, walking back to the dormitory. He begin to smile.

▼

T. D. ALLEN

FROM THE PREFACE TO *MIRACLE HILL*

One day I said, "I think readers would like to know how you first decided you'd like to write. It was during orientation, wasn't it?"

"Yes," Barney (Broneco) answered.

"Well, try to remember all about it," I suggested, "Your readers will want to know how you got started, and you have skipped over that part."

He sat at the long table in our writing studio with a pad of paper before him and his chin in his palm. Finally he asked, "What was that you gave us that day? A kind of seed or something, I think."

. . . In a few minutes, instead of giving me the paragraph
or two I was waiting for to insert in Chapter XV, Barney laid a
short poem on my desk.

"Barney," I scolded, "I thought you were going to help
me fill in. . . ."

"I just wrote this to get wound up," he said.

THE DRIFTING LONELY SEED

From the casein dark-blue sky,
    Through the emptiness of space,
 A sailing wisp of cotton.
    Never have I been so thrilled!
The drifting lonely seed,
    Came past my barred window,
Whirling orbit, it landed before me,
    As though it were a wooly lamb . . .
Untouched, untamed, and alone . . .
    Walked atop my desk, stepping daintily.
Reaching forth my hands, I found you,
    Gentle, weightless, tantalizing.
I blew you out through barricaded window;
    You pranced, circled round me,
Sharing with me your airy freedom.

PART FOUR

SURVIVAL

There have always been the songs, the prayers, the stories. There have always been the voices. There have always been the people. There have always been those words which evoked meaning and the meaning's magical wonder. There has always been the spirit which inspired the desire for life to go on. And it has been through the words of the songs, the prayers, the stories that the people have found a way to continue, for life to go on.

—*Simon J. Ortiz* [8]

And now we begin to experience the circle, the symbol for American Indian beliefs and lifeways—and literature. The beliefs and values with which we began this exploration of Native American literature now forms the link to this final section on survival. The circle is complete and begins again. Everything is interrelated; there is wholeness and harmony.

This is a time of renaissance. Not only have Indians survived, they have changed, adapted, and developed. And they remain uniquely, proudly, ardently Indian. Words have taken new forms, and the oral tradition has been supplemented by the written forms of poetry, novels, biography, and history. But the people, the individuals and their cultures, have survived, and their voices still speak in both old ways and new.

The theme of survival weaves its way through the lives of individuals. Writers speak of people enduring a single day or conquering a personal challenge, and of cultures surviving through the millennia. Survival is seen in political protest and the quest for self-determination. Tribal lands have been restored, hunting and fishing rights regained, and cultural and religious practices, such as the Sun Dance and sweat lodges, have been renewed. Survival is also evident in new forms of literature, art, music, dance, and celebration.

And the voices of American Indian people eloquently remind us of the link between survival and values and beliefs. The people and their literature shall survive.

NILA NORTHSUN

(SHOSHONE-CHIPPEWA)

nila northSun prefers to avoid capital letters in her name and in her writing. She grew up in the San Francisco area and reports that she can't grow vegetables and doesn't like deer meat. Her writing addresses contemporary topics in Indian life and thought.

SOME THOUGHTS

the northwest waits. lush. green. moist, alive. diverse. mountains, valleys, raging rivers, prehistoric ferns, vines entwining, mingling with voices from the past and present. our voices. salmon, carp, skink, eels. grandmother loon. deer, beaver, grandfather raven. coyote, rabbit. us.

our voice. praising, singing, gossiping, telling stories, passing our tradition from one generation to the next. they call it oral tradition. teaching by word of mouth. a good way to share. at one time our brother and sister animals talked. to each other. to us. now we pass on their legends and adventures in our stories, we are part of the land. it is in our songs and prayers. it is part of everyday life. giving and talking with the land. loving. rich dark forests. enjoying.

regions do not have lines drawn by men. then, as now, it is travel and trade. sharing. exchanging.

as our surroundings changed, so did our voice. there are still trees. but there are also logging trucks coming down the road. eagle is almost no more. not many live in willow lodges. TV brightens dark nights. and some of us write.

Moon Walker, by Bert D. Seabourn
(Cherokee ancestry), 1981.

some still have a very tight hold on the more traditional ways. translations and transcriptions take the old ways. put them on paper. songs & prayers. the old stories passed down so as not to be lost or twisted. stories grandmother told them. we write these while sitting at a table. on a typewriter. trying to remember what they said. others write about what we see now. today. semi-urbanized indians. driving around in a pickup. drinking. looking for the way back.

if one were to attempt to find, among the diversity of contemporary indian writing, a major 'thrust' or 'concern,' perhaps it is to reestablish, within a larger society that all but precludes it, a society linked in harmony with the earth . . .

▼

SIMON J. ORTIZ
(ACOMA PUEBLO)

Born and raised in Acoma Pueblo, Simon Ortiz is a poet, short fiction writer, essayist, and recently a filmwriter. He lives at Deetseyamah, a rural community in New Mexico.

SURVIVAL THIS WAY

Survival, I know how this way.
This way, I know.
It rains.
Mountains and canyons and plants
grow.

Woman and Children, by Wa Wa Chaw (Mission), date unknown.

We travelled this way,
gauged our distance by stories
and loved our children.
We taught them
to love their births.
We told ourselves over and over
again, "We shall survive
this way."

▼

N. SCOTT MOMADAY
(KIOWA)

Because of his Pulitzer Prize-winning novel, House Made of Dawn, *N. Scott Momaday is often thought of as the author who finally brought acclaim to American Indian literature. Momaday received his M.A. and Ph.D. from Stanford University and has spent much of his life teaching English and literature.*

THE DELIGHT SONG OF TSOAI-TALEE

I am a feather in the bright sky.
I am the blue horse that runs in the plain.
I am the fish that rolls, shining, in the water.
I am the shadow that follows a child.
I am the evening light, the lustre of meadows.
I am an eagle playing with the wind.
I am a cluster of bright beads.
I am the farthest star.
I am the cold of the dawn.
I am the roaring of the rain.
I am the glitter on the crust of the snow.
I am the long track of the moon in a lake.
I am a flame of the four colors.
I am a deer standing way in the dusk.
I am a field of sumac and the poome blanche.
I am an angle of geese upon the winter sky.
I am the hunger of a young wolf.
I am the whole dream of these things.

I stand in good relation to the earth.
I stand in good relation to the gods.
I stand in good relation to all that is beautiful.
I stand in good relation to the daughter of *Tsen-Tainte.*
You see, I am alive, I am alive.

▼

PHILLIP DEERE
(MUSKOGEE-CREEK)

NO MORE ARE WE GOING TO STAND AROUND. . . .
THIS IS NOT THE END OF THE LONGEST WALK

In July 1978 thousands of Indians from all over the country marched to Washington, D.C., to call attention to the problems of American Indian people and to affirm their unity. Their march was called the Longest Walk. Only part of Phillip Deere's lengthy speech to the demonstrators is presented here.

We are part of nature. Our pipes are red. Our faces, many times, we paint red. But we represent the Creation. We hear about Red Power. There are many definitions to Red Power.

Sometimes we refer to Red as the blood. But all colors of Man have the same color of blood. The fish life, they have blood also. The animals, too, have red blood. Everyone has red blood. But everyone was not made out of the red clay of America.

Only the Indian people are the original people of America. Our roots are buried deep in the soils of America. We are the only people who have continued with the oldest religion in this country. We are the people who still yet speak the languages given to us by the Creator. Our religion has survived, our languages have survived.

Long before this building [*The Capitol*] was built, my ancestors talked the language that I talk today. And I hope to see my Indian people continue to live long after this building crumbles!

I see, in the future, perhaps this civilization is coming near to the end. For that reason, we have continued with the instructions of our ancestors. We are the only people who know how to survive in this country. We have existed here for thousands and thousands of years. The smartest man in America does not know and cannot date the time that we originated.

This is our homeland. We came from no other country. Regardless of how many millions and millions of dollars are spent on an Indian, to make him someone else, all these millions have failed to make a White Man out of the Indian. We are the evidence of the Western Hemisphere!

In the beginning of time, when everything was created, our ancestors also came about in this part of the world. There is no Indian here, on these grounds, that will say that we came across the Bering Straits. There is no Indian standing among us who will say that we descended from apes and monkeys.

We have always looked at ourselves as human beings. In some institutions we are told that man descended from apes and monkeys. I sometimes believe that there are some people that descended from apes and monkeys! That's why in the past two hundred years, there are some people who do not understand what an Indian is.

We are the original people here. No one can tell us how to live here! No one is able to direct our lives! We have forgotten in a short time that when the first people landed on our shores, they could not survive. Even the pilgrims could not survive. The Indians showed them the way of survival. We taught them how to live.

We taught them how to plant corn. That corn was a Tree of Life for us. We showed them that this is life here in America. And they survived.

Not too many years afterwards, foreign agents came to our house and tried to tell us how to farm. Not too many years afterwards, they began to tell us how to live. They began to tell us that our religion was wrong, our way of life was no good. This is not the agreement that we made. This is not the treaty that we made with the U.S. government, or any other country.

We agreed that we would remain as independent nations, that we would be sovereign people. It was understood that these people who were seeking freedom could have their freedom and have the same soil to share here, with us. We had enough room for these people because we lived by an understood law. A law that we had for thousands of years.

We had an unchanging government. The law of love, peace, and respect, no man-made laws will ever take the place of it! And this is the law that we have always lived by.

Because we understood this law, every Indian door was open. Through these doors walked Christopher Columbus. Through these doors walked the Pilgrims, because of that

His Hair Flows Like a River, by T. C. Cannon (Caddo-Kiowa), 1973.

law of love and respect that we had for all human beings.

But times changed. After entering our door, they took advantage of the Native people here. Their greed—we have seen it. Many of our people have died. Many of our people were massacred because they wanted more land. We gave them land through treaties. We gave and we gave, and we have no more to give today!

Not only land was taken. Even the culture, even the religion, under man-made laws, were taken away from the Native people. But we managed to survive. We continued with our way of life.

The jailhouses, the prisons in this country, are no more than four hundred years old. Prior to the coming of Columbus, more than four hundred tribes speaking different languages, having different ways, having different religions, lived here. None of these tribes had jailhouses. They had no prison walls. They had no insane asylums. No country today can exist without them!

Why did we not have any prisons? Why did we not have jailhouses or insane asylums? Because we lived by an understood law.

We understood what life is all about. To this day, we are not confused. My elders, spiritual leaders, medicine men, clan mothers, have no disagreements. We are not that confused. We come to you with one mind. We do not disagree on our religion. I have never tried to convert the Lakota people into Muskogee ways.

The movement of the Indian people will continue to go on. We have been made indestructible. Today the younger generation of my people stands up in pride of the Indian people. This is not the end of The Longest Walk!

We are going to continue to walk, and walk, and walk until we find freedom for all the Native people! And I will remind you, you may not be an Indian, but you better join us. Your life is at stake. Your survival depends on this. Ho!

▼

GAIL TREMBLAY
(ONONDAGA-MICMAC-
FRENCH CANADIAN)

As a mother and poet, an artist and a member of the faculty at The Evergreen State College, Gail Tremblay has been acclaimed by her contemporaries as "a poet of power and clarity" and "a singer of eminent power and grace."

IT IS IMPORTANT

On dark nights, when thoughts fly like nightbirds
looking for prey, it is important to remember
to bless with names every creature that comes
to mind; to sing a thankful song and hold
the magic of the whole creation close in the heart,
to watch light dance and know the sacred is alive.
On dark nights, when owls watch, their eyes
gleaming in the black expanse of starless sky,
it is important to gather the medicine bones,
the eagle feathers, the tobacco bundles, the braided
sweetgrass, the cedar, and the sage, and pray
the world will heal and breath feed the plants
that care for the nations keeping the circle whole.

Beaded Bag with Full Moon,
by Kathryn Stewart (Blackfeet/Crow), 1977.

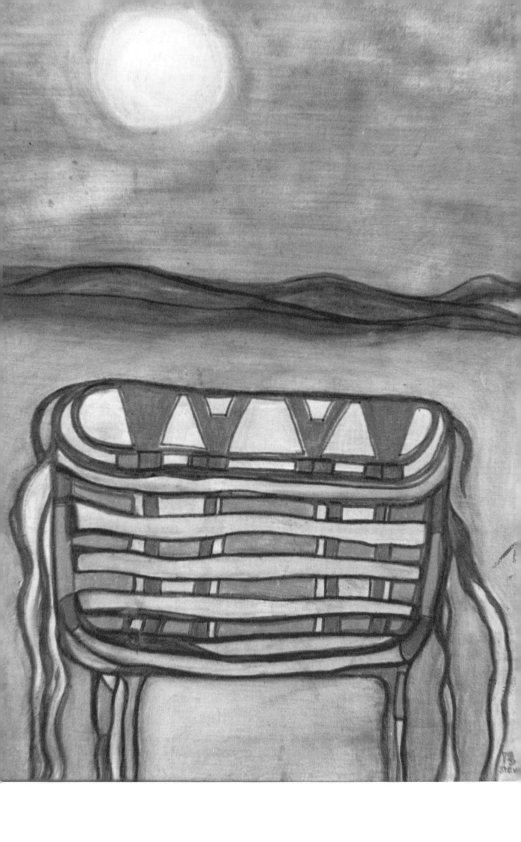

On dark nights, when those who think only of themselves
conjure over stones and sing spells to feed their wills,
it is important to give gifts and to love everything
that shows itself as good. It is time to turn
to the Great Mystery and know the Grandfathers have
mercy on us that we may help the people to survive.
On dark nights, when confusion makes those who envy
hate and curse the winds, face the four directions
and mumble names, it is important to stand
and see that our only work is to give what others
need, that everything that touches us is a holy
gift to teach us we are loved. When sun rises,
and light surrounds life making blessings grow,
it is important to praise its coming, and exhale
letting all we hold inside our lungs travel east
and mix its power with the air; it is important to praise
dawn's power breathing in and know we live in good
relation to all creation and sing what must be sung.

▼

MARILOU AWIAKTA
(CHEROKEE)

*Marilou Awiakta has written for both children and adults;
she brings history alive for children and addresses difficult
issues in her work for adults. As a child, she lived in Oak
Ridge, Tennessee, which she calls an "atomic reservation."
(Oak Ridge was a research site for development of the
atomic bomb.) In this poem, a woman is forced to make a
heartbreaking decision in order to survive.*

WHAT THE CHOCTAW WOMAN SAID

My husband is an alcoholic.
He went to the Veterans' Hospital and said,
"My spirit is sick. I am dying."
They said, "You need tests. Go to the lab."
He came home.
Later he went back and told them again,
"My spirit is sick. I am dying."
"You need meaningful work," they said.
"Go to the social worker."
He came home.
The last time he went they
sent him to a psychiatrist.
When my husband told him, "My spirit is
sick. I am dying," the psychiatrist
said, "What do you mean by 'spirit'?"
My husband came home.
He'll never go back.
My only hope is to get him to
a medicine man
but the great ones are in the West.
I don't have the money to take him.
The trouble is, most people look down
on us and our culture.
It's harder on a man.
It kills his pride.
For a woman it's not as bad.
We have to make sure the children
survive, no matter what.

If I stay with my husband,
the children will get sick in their spirits.
They may die.
I have to leave him.

▼

PAULA GUNN ALLEN
(LAGUNA PUEBLO)

Paula Gunn Allen stresses her mixed ancestry, Laguna and Jewish Lebanese, and its influence upon her writing: "My poetry, my poetics and my aesthetics all arise out of this chaotic mix." Allen is a prominent scholar and prolific contemporary writer of American Indian literature.

KOPIS'TAYA (A GATHERING OF SPIRITS)

Because we live in the browning season
the heavy air blocking our breath,
and in this time when living
is only survival, we doubt the voices
that come shadowed on the air,
that weave within our brains
certain thoughts, a motion that is soft,
imperceptible, a twilight rain
soft feather's fall, a small body
dropping into its nest, rustling, murmuring,
settling in for the night.

Because we live in the hardedged season,
where plastic brittle and gleaming shines
and in this space that is cornered and angled,

we do not notice wet, moist, the significant
drops falling in perfect spheres
that are the certain measures of our minds;
almost invisible, those tears,
soft as dew, fragile, that cling to leaves,
petals, roots, gentle and sure,
every morning.

We are the women of daylight; of clocks and steel
foundries, of drugstores and streetlights,
of superhighways that slice our days in two.
Wrapped around in glass and steel we ride
our lives; behind dark glasses we hide our eyes,
our thoughts, shaded, seem obscure, smoke
fills our minds, whisky husks our songs,
polyester cuts our bodies from our breath,
our feet from the welcoming stones of earth.
Our dreams are pale memories of themselves,
and nagging doubt is the false measure of our days.

Even so, the spirit voices are singing,
their thoughts are dancing in the dirty air.
Their feet touch the cement, the asphalt
delighting, still they weave dreams upon our
shadowed skulls, if we could listen.
If we could hear.
Let's go then. Let's find them. Let's
listen for the water, the careful gleaming drops
that glisten on the leaves, the flowers. Let's
ride the midnight, the early dawn. Feel the wind
striding through our hair. Let's dance
the dance of feathers, the dance of birds.

▼

WILMA MANKILLER (CHEROKEE)

Wilma Mankiller, as the principal chief of the Cherokee Nation of Oklahoma, reflected encouragement, commitment, hope, and survival in her comments on the Columbian Quincentenary.

GUEST ESSAY

Certainly I believe the ancient tribal cultures have important lessons to teach the rest of the world about the interconnectedness of all living things and the simple fact that our existence is dependent upon the natural world we are rapidly destroying. . . .

While it is indisputable that the traditional value systems native people held for centuries before European contact have been somewhat eroded, basic traditional values continue to exist, even in the most fragmented, troubled communities. The traditional value systems that have sustained us throughout the past 500 years of trauma are those value systems that will bolster us and help us enter the 21st century on our own terms.

Despite the last 500 years, there is much to celebrate as we approach 1992. Our languages are still strong, ceremonies that we have been conducting since the beginning of time are still being held, our governments are surviving, and most importantly, we continue to exist as a distinct cultural group in the midst of the most powerful country in the world. Yet we also must recognize that we face a daunting set of problems and issues—continual threats to tribal sovereignty, low educational attainment levels, double digit unemployment, many homes without basic amenities and racism. To grapple with these problems in a positive, forward thinking way, we are beginning to look more to our own people, communities and history for solutions. We have begun to trust our own thinking again. If we are to look to our culture and history for solutions to problems, let us look at an accurate history, not the Columbus myth native children and non-native children are taught in every grade school history class in America.

As native people approach the 21st century, we look into the faces of our youth and see, despite everything, hope. We would like to see that hope kept alive by doing everything possible to assure that our tribal communities continue to dig a way out of the devastation of the past 500 years. We look forward to the next 500 years as a time of renewal and revitalization for native people throughout North America.

▼

BUDDY RED BOW (LAKOTA SIOUX)
AND DIK DARNELL

Buddy Red Bow was a popular singer who died in 1993. He blends rock-and-roll music with lyrics about Indian concerns. In even the most contemporary Indian music, you will hear about beliefs, traditions, change, and survival. This is the title song from Red Bow's last album, Black Hills Dreamer, *which was dedicated to his ancestors.*

BLACK HILLS DREAMER

Born on the reservation,
Abandoned as a child,
Frightened and confused for years,
Searching for a smile.
Dancing with the sun and moon.
I was just sixteen
And I gave my heart to the sacred tree.
Eagle Bear was proud of me.

And I had a dream, inside the crystal cave.
You came to me
And black elk sang this song to me.
Thunderbird overhead I see
And the eagle bone was whistling thru the night.
Paha paha sapa, paha paha sapa.

I'm a black hills dreamer,
I'm a black hills dreamer,
I'm a black hills dreamer going home, going home.

It makes my heart feel good
Seeing people on this old red road
Going back to mother earth again
And with the children I will make my stand
The black hills are the sacred ground
"We'll always love this land."

And I had a dream
Standing on this mountain I could see
The elders looking back on me
Horses in the sky I see
Flaming spears are falling down on me.

I'm a black hills dreamer,
I'm a black hills dreamer,
I'm a black hills dreamer going home, going home.

At the conclusion of the song Buddy prays in Lakota: "*Oh Great Spirit and Grandmother Earth, on this night we came to pray. We want our people to live, that is why we're praying. The Thunderbirds that are flying over us tonight, they are watching over us. The little boys and girls will live, that's what I pray for. Hear us.*"

▼

LOUISE ERDRICH (OJIBWAY)

"The Red Convertible" is a chapter from the book Love Medicine, *which has been called Louise Erdrich's masterpiece. In many ways each chapter of this book, like "The Red Convertible," can stand alone. Erdrich has written three books that present the intertwined stories of an intriguing Indian family living on the Turtle Mountain Reservation in North Dakota. In describing* Love Medicine, *Kenneth Lincoln writes, "Indians . . . go on in the special ethos of pride and defeat and survival, the estrangement of America's first peoples, reserved inside history, clawing their ways home, hanging on, making pies and waxing wood floors and hunting geese and wiring tractors together, like the rest of rural working America, but with that added inflection of pain, desperation, humor, another aboriginal tongue and cultural heritage, and immeasurable enduring strength that is 'native' American—the ache of self-definition and going on, in the face of all odds.*"[9]

THE RED CONVERTIBLE

I was the first one to drive a convertible on my reservation. And of course it was red, a red Olds. I owned that car along with my brother Henry Junior. We owned it together until his boots filled with water on a windy night and he bought out my share. Now Henry owns the whole car, and his younger brother Lyman (that's myself), Lyman walks everywhere he goes.

How did I earn enough money to buy my share in the first place? My one talent was I could always make money. I had a touch for it, unusual in a Chippewa. From the first I was different that way, and everyone recognized it. I was the only kid they let in the American Legion Hall to shine shoes, for example, and one Christmas I sold spiritual bouquets for the mission door to door. The nuns let me keep a percentage. Once I started, it seemed the more money I made the easier the money came. Everyone encouraged it. When I was fifteen I got a job washing dishes at the Joliet Cafe, and that was where my first big break happened.

It wasn't long before I was promoted to bussing tables, and then the short-order cook quit and I was hired to take her place. No sooner than you know it I was managing the Joliet. The rest is history. I went on managing. I soon became part owner, and of course there was no stopping me then. It wasn't long before the whole thing was mine.

After I'd owned the Joliet for one year, it blew over in the worse tornado ever seen around here. The whole operation was smashed to bits. A total loss. The fryalator was up in a tree, the grill torn in half like it was paper. I was only sixteen. I had it all in my mother's name, and I lost it quick, but before I lost it I had every one of my relatives, and their relatives, to dinner, and I also bought that red Olds I mentioned, along with Henry.

The first time we saw it! I'll tell you when we first saw it. We had gotten a ride up to Winnipeg, and both of us had money. Don't ask me why, because we never mentioned a car or anything, we just had all our money. Mine was cash, a big bankroll from the Joliet's insurance. Henry had two checks—a week's extra pay for being laid off, and his regular check from the Jewel Bearing Plant.

We were walking down Portage anyway, seeing the sights, when we saw it. There it was, parked, large as life. Really as *if* it was alive. I thought of the word *repose*, because the car wasn't simply stopped, parked, or whatever. That car reposed, calm and gleaming, a FOR SALE sign in its left front window. Then, before we had thought it over at all, the car belonged to us and our pockets were empty. We had just enough money for gas back home.

We went places in that car, me and Henry. We took off driving all one whole summer. We started off toward the Little Knife River and Mandaree in Fort Berthold and then we found ourselves down in Wakpala somehow, and then suddenly we were over in Montana on the Rocky Boys, and yet the summer was not even half over. Some people hang on to details when they travel, but we didn't let them bother us and just lived our everyday lives here to there.

I do remember this one place with willows. I remember I laid under those trees and it was comfortable. So comfortable. The branches bent down all around me like a tent or a stable. And quiet, it was quiet, even though there was a powwow close enough so I could see it going on. The air was not too still, not too windy either. When the dust rises up and hangs in the air around the dancers like that, I feel good. Henry was asleep with his arms thrown wide. Later on, he woke up and we started driving again. We were somewhere in Montana, or maybe on the Blood Reserve—it could have been anywhere. Anyway it was where we met the girl.

All her hair was in buns around her ears, that's the first thing I noticed about her. She was posed alongside the road with her arm out, so we stopped. That girl was short, so short her lumber shirt looked comical on her, like a nightgown. She had jeans on and fancy moccasins and she carried a little suitcase.

"Hop on in," says Henry. So she climbs in between us.

"We'll take you home," I says. "Where do you live?"

"Chicken," she says.

"Where the hell's that?" I ask her.

"Alaska."

"Okay," says Henry, and we drive.

We got up there and never wanted to leave. The sun doesn't truly set there in summer, and the night is more a soft dusk. You might doze off, sometimes, but before you know it you're up again, like an animal in nature. You never feel like you have to sleep hard or put away the world. And things would grow up there. One day just dirt or moss, the next day flowers and long grass. The girl's name was Susy. Her family really took to us. They fed us and put us up. We had our own tent to live in by their house, and the kids would be in and out of there all day and night. They couldn't get over me and Henry being brothers, we looked so different. We told them we knew we had the same mother, anyway.

One night Susy came in to visit us. We sat around in the tent talking of this thing and that. The season was changing. It was getting darker by that time, and the cold was even getting just a little mean. I told her it was time for us to go. She stood up on a chair.

"You never seen my hair," Susy said.

That was true. She was standing on a chair, but still, when she unclipped her buns the hair reached all the way to the ground. Our eyes opened. You couldn't tell how much hair she had when it was rolled up so neatly. Then my brother Henry did something funny. He went up to the chair and said, "Jump on my shoulders." So she did that, and her hair reached down past his waist, and he started twirling, this way and that, so her hair was flung out from side to side.

"I always wondered what it was like to have long pretty hair" Henry says. Well, we laughed. It was a funny sight, the way he did it. The next morning we got up and took leave of those people.

On to greener pastures, as they say. It was down through Spokane and across Idaho then Montana and very soon we were racing the weather right along under the Canadian border through Columbus, Des Lacs, and then we were in Bottineau Country and soon home. We'd made most of the trip, that summer, without putting up the car hood at all. We got home just in time, it turned out, for the army to remember Henry had signed up to join it.

I don't wonder that the army was so glad to get my brother that they turned him into a Marine. He was built like a brick outhouse anyway. We liked to tease him that they really wanted him for his Indian nose. He had a nose big and sharp as a hatchet, like the nose on Red Tomahawk, the Indian who killed Sitting Bull, whose profile is on signs all along the North Dakota highways. Henry went off to training camp, came home once during Christmas, then the next thing you know we got an overseas letter from him. It was 1970, and he said he was stationed up in the northern hill country. Whereabouts I did not know. He wasn't such a hot letter writer, and only got off two before the enemy caught him. I could never keep it straight, which direction those good Vietnam soldiers were from.

I wrote him back several times, even though I didn't know if those letters would get through. I kept him informed all about the car. Most of the time I had it up on blocks in the yard or half taken apart, because that long trip did a hard job on it under the hood.

I always had good luck with numbers, and never worried about the draft myself. I never even had to think about what my number was. But Henry was never lucky in the same way as me. It was at least three years before Henry came home. By then I guess the whole war was solved in the government's mind, but for him it would keep on going. In those years I'd put his car into almost perfect shape. I always thought of it as his car while he was gone, even though when he left he said, "Now it's yours," and threw me his key.

"Thanks for the extra key," I'd said. "I'll put it up in your drawer just in case I need it." He laughed.

When he came home, though, Henry was very different, and I'll say this; the change was no good. You could hardly expect him to change for the better, I know. But he was quiet, so quiet, and never comfortable sitting still anywhere but always up and moving around. I thought back to times we'd sit still for whole afternoons, never moving a muscle, just shifting our weight along the ground, talking to whoever sat with us, watching things. He'd always had a joke then, too, and now you couldn't get him to laugh, or when he did it was more the sound of a man choking, a sound that stopped up the throats of other people around him. They got to leaving him alone most of the time, and I didn't blame them. It was a fact: Henry was jumpy and mean.

I'd bought a color TV set for my mom and the rest of us while Henry was away. Money still came very easy. I was sorry I'd ever bought it though, because of Henry. I was also sorry I'd bought color because with black-and-white the pictures seem older and farther away. But what are you going to do? He sat in front of it, watching it, and that was the only time he was completely still. But it was the kind of stillness that you see in a rabbit when it freezes and before it will bolt. He was not easy. He sat in his chair gripping the armrest with all his might, as if the chair itself was moving at a high speed and if he let go at all he would rocket forward and maybe crash right through the set.

Once I was in the room watching TV with Henry and I heard his teeth click at something. I looked over, and he'd bitten through his lip. Blood was going down his chin. I tell you right then I wanted to smash that tube to pieces. I went over to it but Henry must have known what I was up to. He rushed from his chair and shoved me out of the way, against the wall. I told myself he didn't know what he was doing.

My mom came in, turned the set off real quiet, and told us she had made something for supper. So we went and sat down. There was still blood going down Henry's chin, but he didn't notice it and no one said anything, even though every time he took a bite of his bread his blood fell onto it until he was eating his own blood mixed in the food.

While Henry was not around we talked about what was going to happen to him. There were no Indian doctors on the reservation, and my mom was afraid of trusting Old Man Pillager because he courted her long ago and was jealous of her husbands. He might take revenge through her son. We were afraid that if we brought Henry to a regular hospital they would keep him.

"They don't fix them in those places," Mom said; "they just give them drugs."

"We wouldn't get him there in the first place," I agreed, "so let's just forget about it."

Then I thought about the car.

Henry had not even looked at the car since he'd gotten home, though like I said, it was in tip-top condition and ready to drive. I thought the car might bring the old Henry back somehow. So I bided my time and waited for my chance to interest him in the vehicle.

One night Henry was off somewhere. I took myself a hammer. I went out to that car and I did a number on its underside. Whacked it up. Bent the tail pipe double. Ripped the muffler loose. By the time I was done with the car it looked worse than any typical Indian car that has been driven all its life on reservation roads, which they always say are like government promises—full of holes. It just about hurt me, I'll tell you that! I threw dirt in the carburetor and I ripped all the electric tape off the seats. I made it look just as beat up as I could. Then I sat back and waited for Henry to find it.

Still, it took him over a month. That was all right, because it was just getting warm enough, not melting, but warm enough to work outside.

"Lyman," he says, walking in one day, "that red car looks like shit."

"Well it's old," I says. "You got to expect that."

"No way!" says Henry. "That car's a classic! But you went and ran the piss right out of it, Lyman, and you know it don't deserve that. I kept that car in A-one shape. You don't remember. You're too young. But when I left, that car was running like a watch. Now I don't even know if I can get it to start again, let alone get it anywhere near its old condition."

"Well you try," I said, like I was getting mad, "but I say it's a piece of junk."

Then I walked out before he could realize I knew he'd strung together more than six words at once.

After that I thought he'd freeze himself to death working on that car. He was out there all day, and at night he rigged up a little lamp, ran a cord out the window, and had himself some light to see by while he worked. He was better than he had been before, but that's still not saying much. It was easier for him to do the things the rest of us did. He ate more slowly and didn't jump up and down during the meal to get this or that or look out the window. I put my hand in the back of the TV set, I admit, and fiddled around with it good, so that it was almost impossible now to get a clear picture.

He didn't look at it very often anyway. He was always out with that car or going off to get parts for it. By the time it was really melting outside, he had it fixed.

I had been feeling down in the dumps about Henry around this time. We had always been together before. Henry and Lyman. But he was such a loner now that I didn't know how to take it. So I jumped at the chance one day when Henry seemed friendly. It's not that he smiled or anything. He just said, "Let's take that old shitbox for a spin." Just the way he said it made me think he could be coming around.

We went out to the car. It was spring. The sun was shining very bright. My only sister, Bonita, who was just eleven years old, came out and made us stand together for a picture. Henry leaned his elbow on the red car's windshield, and he took his other arm and put it over my shoulder, very carefully, as though it was heavy for him to lift and he didn't want to bring the weight down all at once.

"Smile," Bonita said, and he did.

That picture. I never look at it anymore. A few months ago, I don't know why, I got his picture out and tacked it on the wall. I felt good about Henry at the time, close to him. I felt good having his picture on the wall, until one night when I was looking at television. I was a little drunk and stoned. I looked up at the wall and Henry was staring at me. I don't know what it was, but his smile had changed, or maybe it was gone. All I know is I couldn't stay in the same room with that picture. I was shaking. I got up, closed the door, and went into the kitchen. A little later my friend Ray came over and we both went back into that room. We put the picture in a brown bag, folded the bag over and over tightly, then put it way back in a closet.

I still see the picture now, as if it tugs at me, whenever I pass that closet door. The picture is very clear in my mind. It was so sunny that day Henry had to squint against the glare. Or maybe the camera Bonita held flashed like a mirror, blinding him, before she snapped the picture. My face is right out in the sun, big and round. But he might have drawn back, because the shadows on his face are deep as holes. There are two shadows curved like little hooks around the ends of his smile, as if to frame it and try to keep it there— that one, first smile that looked like it might have hurt his face. He has his field jacket on and the worn-in clothes he'd come back in and kept wearing ever since. After Bonita took the picture, she went into the house and we got into the car. There was a full cooler in the trunk. We started off, east, toward Pembina and the Red River because Henry said he wanted to see the high water.

The trip over there was beautiful. When everything starts changing, drying up, clearing off, you feel like your whole life is starting. Henry felt it, too. The top was down and the car hummed like a top. He'd really put it back in shape, even the tape on the seats was very carefully put down and glued back in layers. It's not that he smiled again or even joked, but his face looked to me as if it was clear, more peaceful. It looked as though he wasn't thinking of anything in particular except the bare fields and windbreaks and houses we were passing.

The river was high and full of winter trash when we got there. The sun was still out, but it was colder by the river.

There were still little clumps of dirty snow here and there on the banks. The water hadn't gone over the banks yet, but it would, you could tell. It was just at its limit, hard swollen, glossy like an old gray scar. We made ourselves a fire, and we sat down and watched the current go. As I watched it I felt something squeezing inside me and tightening and trying to let go all at the same time. I knew I was not just feeling it myself; I knew I was feeling what Henry was going through at that moment. Except that I couldn't stand it, the closing and opening. I jumped to my feet. I took Henry by the shoulders and I stared shaking him. "Wake up," I says, "wake up, wake up, wake up!" I didn't know what had come over me. I sat down beside him again.

His face was totally white and hard. Then it broke, like stones break all of a sudden when water boils up inside them.

"I know it," he says. "I know it. I can't help it. It's no use."

We start talking. He said he knew what I'd done with the car. It was obvious it had been whacked out of shape and not just neglected. He said he wanted to give the car to me for good now, it was no use. He said he'd fixed it just to give it back and I should take it.

"No way," I says, "I don't want it."

"That's okay," he says, "you take it."

"I don't want it, though," I says back to him, and then to emphasize, just to emphasize, you understand, I touch his shoulder. He slaps my hand off.

"Take that car," he says.

"No," I say, "make me," I say, and then he grabs my jacket and rips the arm loose. That jacket is a class act, suede with tags and zippers. I push Henry backwards, off the log. He jumps up and bowls me over. We go down in a clinch and come up swinging hard, for all we're worth, with our fists. He socks my jaw so hard I feel like it swings loose. Then I'm at his ribcage and land a good one under his chin so his head snaps back. He's dazzled. He looks at me and I look at him and then his eyes are full of tears and blood and at first I think he's crying. But no, he's laughing. "Ha! Ha!' he says. "Ha! Ha! Take good care of it."

"Okay," I says, "okay, no problem. Ha! Ha!"

I can't help it, and I start laughing, too. My face feels fat and strange, and after a while I get a beer from the cooler in the trunk, and when I hand it to Henry he takes his shirt and wipes my germs off. "Hoof-and-mouth disease," he says. For some reason this cracks me up, and so we're really laughing for a while, and then we drink all the rest of the beers one by one and throw them in the river and see how far, how fast, the current takes them before they fill up and sink.

"You want to go on back?" I ask after a while. "Maybe we could snag a couple nice Kashpaw girls."

He says nothing. But I can tell his mood is turning again.

"They're all crazy, the girls up here, every damn one of them."

"You're crazy too," I say, to jolly him up. "Crazy Lamartine boys!"

He looks as though he will take this wrong at first. His face twists, then clears, and he jumps up on his feet. "That's right!" he says. "Crazier 'n hell. Crazy Indians!"

I think it's the old Henry again. He throws off his jacket

and starts swinging his legs out from the knees like a fancy dancer. He's down doing something between a grouse dance and a bunny hop, no kind of dance I ever saw before, but neither has anyone else on all this green growing earth. He's wild. He wants to pitch whoopee! He's up and at me and all over. All this time I'm laughing so hard, so hard my belly is getting tied up in a knot.

"Got to cool me off!" he shouts all of a sudden. Then he runs over to the river and jumps in.

There's boards and other things in the current. It's so high. No sound comes from the river after the splash he makes, so I run right over. I look around. It's getting dark. I see he's halfway across the water already, and I know he didn't swim there but the current took him. It's far. I hear his voice, though, very clearly across it.

"My boots are filling," he says.

He says this in a normal voice, like he just noticed and he doesn't know what to think of it. Then he's gone. A branch comes by. Another branch. And I go in.

By the time I get out of the river, off the snag I pulled myself onto, the sun is down. I walk back to the car, turn on the high beams, and drive it up the bank. I put it in first gear and then I take my foot off the clutch. I get out, close the door, and watch it plow softly into the water. The headlights reach in as they go down, searching, still lighted even after the water swirls over the back end. I wait. The wires short out. It is all finally dark. And then there is only the water, the sound of it going and running and going and running and running.

▼

JOY HARJO (CREEK)

Joy Harjo was born in Tulsa, Oklahoma, in 1951. She was not brought up as a traditional Creek, but she has said that when she writes "there is an old Creek within me that often participates." Responsibility, particularly as a contemporary Indian woman, is a theme that recurs in her writing.

UNTITLED

I feel strongly that I have a responsibility to all
the sources that I am: to all past and future ancestors,
to my home country, to all places that I touch down
on and that are myself, to all voices, all women, all
of my tribe, all people, all earth and beyond that to
all beginnings and endings. In a strange kind of sense
it frees me to believe in myself, to be able to speak,
to have voice, because I have to; it is my survival.

▼

GEORGE HORSE CAPTURE
(GROS VENTRE)

POWWOW

As he does everywhere, the Great Spirit in his infinite wisdom bestows a balance here, too. So, if there is a bad part, there is also a good part. It's good being Indian. As we drive across the country and see the trees and coulees and the

sage brush and grass covering the prairie, we know this is Indian country, and long ago buffalo covered it from horizon to horizon. We know this has always been our land. We will never emigrate to the British Isles or to Australia or to anywhere. This is our home, good or bad. It is our earth and these hills are our hills. It doesn't matter who owns the deed to the land, because these paper holders change and they will always change. But these hills and mountains and valleys and coulees and bluffs are ours, the Indian people's. They have always been ours and they always will be. We know this. It makes us feel good. No one can change this, and it does not matter if we are poor or not. . . . We know where we came from and we know where we are going to be buried. We have a center to our lives. Out of all this chaos, there is a certain order.

Victory Dance, by Oscar Howl (Yanktonai Sioux), 1954.

Notes

1. Velie, Alan, ed., *American Indian Literature: An Anthology* (Norman: University of Oklahoma Press, 1991), p. 83.

2. Harvey, Karen D., Harjo, Lisa D. and Jackson, J., *Teaching About Native Americans* (Washington, D.C.: National Council for the Social Studies, 1990).

3. Fire, John/Lame Deer and Richard Erdoes, *Lame Deer: Seeker of Visions* (New York: Simon & Schuster, Inc., 1976).

4. Boham, Russell V. *Oral Tradition*, in J.D. Blanche, ed., *Native American Reader* (Juneau, Ala.: Denali Press), p. 224.

5. Allen, Paula Gunn, *Studies in American Literature* (New York: Modern Language Association, 1983), p. 11.

6. Allen, Paula Gunn, in Joseph Bruchac, ed., *Survival This Way* (Tucson, Ariz.: Sun Tracks and the University of Arizona Press, 1987), p. 5.

7. Harvey, Karen, and Lisa Harjo. *Indian Country: A History of Native People in America* (Golden, Colo.: North American Press, 1994).

8. Ortiz, Simon J., ed., *Earth Power Coming* (Tsaile, Ariz.: Navajo Community College, 1983), p. vii.

9. Lincoln, Kenneth, *Native American Renaissance* (Berkeley, Cal.: University of California Press, 1983), p. xiii.

Acknowledgments

Alan Velie: "Opening Prayer of the Sun Dance" and "Song Concerning a Message from Washington." From *American Indian Literature* by Alan Velie. Copyright © 1979 by the University of Oklahoma Press.

John Fire/Lame Deer and Richard Erdoes: *Lame Deer: Seeker of Visions.* Copyright © 1976 by John Fire/Lame Deer and Richard Erdoes. Reprinted by permission of Simon & Schuster, Inc.

Russell V. Boham: "Oral Tradition." Native American Reader, edited by J.D. Blanche. Copyright © 1990 by Denali Press. Reprinted by permission of the publisher.

Joy Harjo: "Remember." *That's What She Said*, edited by R. Green. Copyright © 1984 by the Indiana University Press. Reprinted by permission of the publisher.

"A Navajo Night Chant." *Four Masterworks of American Indian Literature*, edited by J. Bierhorst. Reprinted by permission of the author.

Richard Erdoes and Alfonso Ortiz: "Creation of First Man and First Woman." *American Indian Myths and Legends.* Copyright © 1984 by Richard Erdoes and Alfonso Ortiz. Reprinted by permission of Pantheon Books, a division of Random House, Inc.

John G. Neihardt: *Black Elk Speaks.* Reprinted by permission of the author.

Petalesharo: "It Is too Soon, My Great Father, to Send Those Good Men Among Us." From Indian Oratory: Famous Speeches by Noted Indian Chieftains, compiled by W.C. Vanderwerth. Copyright © 1971 by the University of Oklahoma Press. Reprinted by permission of the publisher.

Rayna Green, ed.: *That's What She Said*. Copyright © 1984 by the University of Indiana Press. Reprinted by permission of the publisher.

Emerson Blackhorse Mitchell and T.D. Allen: *Miracle Hill: The Story of a Navajo Boy*. Copyright © 1967 by the University of Oklahoma Press.

Simon J. Ortiz, ed.: *Earth Power Coming*. Reprinted by permission of the author.

Simon J. Ortiz: "Survival This Way." *The Remembered Earth*, edited by J. Bruchac. Reprinted by permission of the author.

Phillip Deere: "No More Are We Going to Stand Around. . . ." *Akwesasne Notes*, edited by J.D. Blanche. Copyright © 1990 by the Mohawk Nation at Akwesasne. Reprinted by permission of the publisher.

Gail Trembly: "It Is Important." *Indian Singing in the Twentieth Century*, edited by A. Lerner. Reprinted from *Indian Singing in the Twentieth Century* (Calyx Books, 1990) by permission of the publisher.

Marilou Awiakta: "What the Choctaw Woman Said." *Through Indian Eyes: The Native Experience in Books for Children*, edited by B. Slapin and D. Seale. Copyright © 1992 by New Society Publications. Reprinted by permission of the publisher.

Paula Gunn Allen: "Kopis'taya." *That's What She Said*, edited by R. Green. Copyright © 1984 by the Indiana University Press. Reprinted by permission of the publisher.

Wilma Mankiller: "Guest Essay." Copyright © 1991 by *Native Peoples*. Reprinted by permission of the publisher.

Buddy Red Bow: "Black Hills Dreamer." *Black Hills Dreamer*, Takanka Records. Written by Buddy Red Bow and Dik Darnell.

Further Reading

Allen, Paula Gunn, *Spider Woman's Granddaughters*. New York: Fawcett Columbine, 1989.

Bruchac, Joseph. *Dawn Land*. Golden, CO: Fulcrum, 1993.

Bruchac, Joseph. *Songs From This Earth on Turtle's Back*. Greenfield Center, NY: Greenfield Review Press, 1983.

Coltelli, L. *Winged Words: American Indian Writers Speak*. Lincoln: University of Nebraska Press, 1990.

Deloria, V., Jr. *Custer Died for Your Sins*. Norman: University of Oklahoma Press, 1969.

Dorris, Michael *A Yellow Raft in Blue Water*. New York: Warner Books, 1988.

Erdoes, Richard, and Alfonso Ortiz. *American Indian Myths and Legends*. New York: Pantheon, 1984.

Erdrich, Louise. *Love Medicine*. New York: Holt, Rinehart & Winston, 1984.

Green, Rayna. *That's What She Said: Contemporary Poetry and Fiction by Native American Women*. Bloomington: University of Indiana Press, 1984.

Hirschfelder, Arlene B., and Beverly R. Singer, *Rising Voices: Writings of Young Native Americans*. New York: Charles Scribner's Sons, 1992.

Koller, J., C. Arnett, S. Nemirow, and P. Blue Cloud, *Coyote's Journal*. Berkeley, CA: Wingbow, 1982.

Lame Deer/John Fire, and Richard Erdoes. *Lame Deer: Seeker of Visions.* New York: Pocket Books, 1972.

Momaday, N. Scott. *House Made of Dawn.* New York: Harper & Row, 1968.

Niehardt, John G. *Black Elk Speaks.* New York: Pocket Books, 1973.

Ortiz, Simon J. *Woven Stone.* Tucson: University of Arizona Press, 1992.

Riley, Patricia. *Growing Up Native American.* New York: William Morrow, 1993.

Silko, Leslie. *Ceremony.* New York: Viking, 1977.

Standing Bear, Luther. *Land of the Spotted Eagle* (reprint). Lincoln: University of Nebraska Press, 1978.

Tapahonso, Luci. *Saanii Dahataal: The Women Are Singing.* Tucson: University of Arizona Press, 1993.

Tremblay, Gail. *Indian Singing in 20th-Century America.* Norman: University of Oklahoma Press, 1989.

Vanderwerth, W. C. *Indian Oratory* (6th printing). Norman: University of Oklahoma Press, 1989.

Velie, Alan. *The Lightning Within: An Anthology of Contemporary American Indian Fiction.* Lincoln: University of Nebraska Press, 1991.

Welch, James. *The Death of Jim Loney* (reprint). New York: Penguin, 1987.

Index